Struggle
TO
Strength

STRUGGLE TO STRENGTH

How Authentic, Relatable Leadership Shapes Success

Jonathan Eldridge

Published by Game Changer Publishing

Paperback ISBN: 978-1-969372-05-6
Hardcover ISBN: 978-1-969372-06-3
Digital ISBN: 978-1-969372-07-0

www.GameChangerPublishing.com

I would like to dedicate this book to my amazing wife, Danielle and our two young men, Tristan and Logan.

My family is my muse, my source for inspiration.
With all my heart, I love you guys!
Thanks for supporting me, believing in me,
and generally just putting up with me:)

Read This First

Just to say thanks for buying and reading my book,
I would like to connect!

Scan the QR Code Here:

Struggle _{TO} Strength

HOW AUTHENTIC,
RELATABLE LEADERSHIP
SHAPES SUCCESS

Jonathan Eldridge

Table of Contents

Introduction: Where Authentic and Relatable Collide!....................................... 1

Chapter 1: It All Starts With Consistency! 9

Chapter 2: Do People Really Know How Much You Care? 21

Chapter 3: Curiosity, It's About Building Trust!............................. 31

Chapter 4: Approachable: What's your Mindset 41

Chapter 5: Authenticity: The Currency of Today 51

Chapter 6: Adaptable: Tackling the Day-to-Day............................... 61

Chapter 7: Respect: It's Unconditional and Should Go Without Saying 71

Chapter 8: Reliable: It Can Make or Break You................................. 81

Chapter 9: Relatable: Do You Understand Your Audience? 89

Chapter 10: Enthusiastic: Are You Living the Day? 99

Chapter 11: Execution: Are You Doing What You Said You Would?..........107

Chapter 12: Eagerness: Can Clients See Your Sense of Urgency?................117

Conclusion: Let's Wrap This in a Bow! 123

INTRODUCTION

Where Authentic and Relatable Collide!

Well, hello world!

My name is Jonathan Eldridge, and it's about time I put pen to paper. It's time to lay it all out there: the good, the bad, the amazing, the risks, and the failures.

Let me be the first to tell you: I am *not* a perfect human. Not even close. I work on myself daily.

What I am, however, is someone experienced in the art of learning from life. From completely starting over, navigating massive grief, sadness, and struggle, to managing colossal organizational stress, I've been through it all. Yet somehow, I've come out the other side stronger and wiser.

I've learned that in human connection, being your true self matters. And when you master my twelve-attribute "CARE Framework" (which I'll proudly shout from a mountaintop), you start being remembered, for all the right reasons.

I've been teaching this CARE Framework, which I've coined "Human Improvement," for several years. These attributes have catapulted my life both personally and professionally. I realized that these attributes are the true differentiators in this world, not the glossy brochure or the sales guy you can smell coming a mile away.

And now, I couldn't be more excited to bring it to you.

Below is my twelve-attribute **CARE Framework,** which I'll break down in detail throughout each chapter.

So strap in. Let's go.

SOULFOCUS
JONATHAN ELDRIDGE

C	**CONSISTENT** Must Be	**COMPASSION** Must Show	**CURIOSITY** Must Have
A	**APPROACHABLE** Mindset	**AUTHENTIC** You	**ADAPTABLE** Industry Day-to-Day
R	**RESPECT** Unconditional	**RELIABLE** 24/7/365	**RELATABLE** Understand Audience
E	**ENTHUSIASTIC** Live the Day	**EXECUTION** Do As You Say	**EAGERNESS** Sense of Urgency

My life has seen triumphant highs and some terrible, often lonely, lows. I've spent years digging and clawing to build staffing markets from nothing, pouring in all the blood, sweat, and tears it takes to create a business from the ground up. That journey, while incredible, has been bumpy to say the least.

I've faced numerous challenges: the death of a sibling, the more recent loss of my father, struggles with addiction and binge drinking, four total knee replacements (yes, you read that right, four), and even a brief cancer scare.

And yet, through it all, these experiences have shaped a truly amazing life, one I now share with a wonderful wife and two incredible kids.

I wrote this book not only for leaders, but for anyone out there who's struggling and is struggling with a plan to move forward. It's for those who feel pressured to conform to societal norms and follow the same old path, instead of listening to their own inner compass.

This book is the culmination of twenty-seven years of professional experience, twenty-five of them in a leadership position, but more importantly, fifty years of learning how to navigate life and continually striving to become a better human.

Additionally, I wanted to define what "world-class" truly should mean. It's a term that often sounds impressive, but at its core, it represents the twelve key attributes outlined above and throughout this book.

To provide a world-class experience means to care more than anyone else in your industry and leave a lasting impression that makes people want to return. It's not just about what you sell; it's about how you make someone feel during the process.

Mastering these twelve attributes enables you to enter a flow state, where you're tapping into your best qualities to create one meaningful, lasting impression.

As you can see in the diagram, each attribute in this framework is assigned one point, making the CARE system a twelve-point model, with one point for every attribute.

Most leaders tend to excel in eight, nine, or even ten of these attributes. While they may always be working on one or two areas for improvement, true transformation happens when all twelve are successfully incorporated into a conversation and demonstrated consistently.

When that happens, you enter a flow state, a powerful zone where communication feels natural, connected, and impactful. These flow-state conversations are where genuine partnerships are formed, and where people are remembered not just for the actions they've taken, but also for the ones they are about to take.

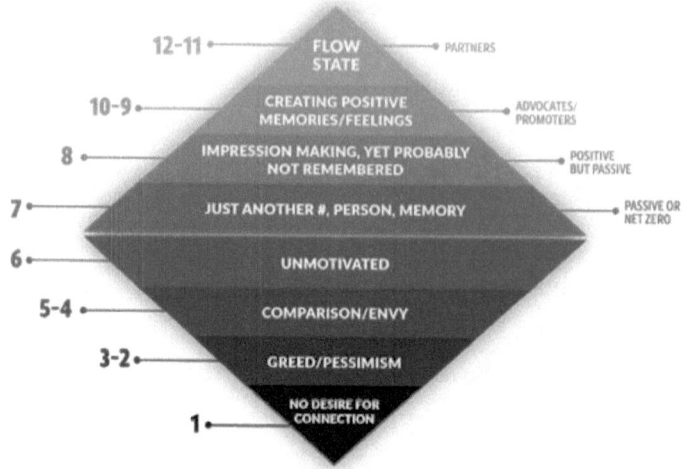

Moreover, this book is for anyone looking to develop their emotional intelligence (EQ), an essential skill that is often overlooked in our educational systems. While high schools have recently added finance courses to the curriculum, there's still a noticeable lack of coursework focused on EQ: how to interact with people, build consistency, show compassion, and demonstrate respect. This book addresses those gaps.

Traditional education might teach you how to create a product, but it doesn't prepare you to land an interview, recover from mistakes, or face adversity. This book will. While I'm not going to focus on AI throughout this entire book, I can tell you that AI can solve your business problems, but it can't solve the human ones. *Trust* beats *tools* when it comes to AI. Human connection creates influence that AI can't generate. Furthermore, relatability drives collaboration (a distinctly human action), and being authentic builds long-term loyalty. These are just a few of the attributes I'll cover in this book: things AI can "describe" but can't carry out.

It's also for anyone grappling with their identity or feeling stuck in life's version of quicksand. There is nothing in life you can't overcome if you commit to living each day to its fullest.

Why should you read/listen to this book? Because, like you, I'm still on a journey of self-improvement. This is a book about growth. Life is a continuous process of becoming better. You should never rest on your laurels or grow complacent with where you are. A "whatever it takes" mentality is something you should carry with you always. As you read, you'll discover that this mindset has been a driving force in my life. The question is: where does it show up in yours?

I want readers to understand that challenge and struggle can lead to strength. Everything you go through, even the parts you feel tempted to hide, can be transformed into something powerful: a way to help others grow. This book encourages vulnerability and the courage to share your experiences.

Ultimately, this book is designed to help you gain clarity about who you are, who you want to become, and what you aspire to achieve.

Make no mistake: whatever you truly want should not come easily. It should stretch you, test you, and sometimes even break you. Without challenges, it may not be worth pursuing at all. Greatness isn't found at the finish line, but in the daily effort, the grit it takes to keep going.

You won't read this book and instantly become great. That's not the expectation. But as you move through it, you'll come to see that life is meant to be lived in the now, not by obsessing over the past through your rear-view mirror, nor by rushing too far ahead on the road. Life is about discovering your true north, your personal compass guiding you toward a truly enriched and meaningful life.

Greatness is found in the pursuit itself, not in the title of being great. It's not about perfection, it's about the purpose. I hope you enjoy this book and the chapters that guide you in building your own "Core CARE Equation."

My current Core CARE Equation consists of: *compassion, authenticity, reliability,* and *enthusiasm.* I say *current* because life changes, and with it, your mindset and focus will evolve.

To give you an example: I used to struggle with consistency and execution. But through rediscovering my passion and fully believing in my framework, I now lean on those two attributes more than ever.

That is my Core CARE Equation. After reading this book, you'll be able to define your own and share it with others. You'll also uncover your premier attribute: the unique talent or trait that's been gifted to you alone, something no one else on earth can replicate in quite the same way.

Spoiler alert: mine is Authenticity.

This uniqueness is what sets you apart. And that's the essence of this book: to help you embrace what makes you different and allow your light to shine. I hope you enjoy the journey.

What's even more exciting is you'll be able to uncover the attributes that need the most improvement; ah, yes, this book will help you in the areas that you struggle with the most. Moreover, my CARE Framework will give you the "Soul Focus" and tools needed to improve on those weaker attributes every day!

Spoiler alert: mine is Adaptable.

So, how do you achieve a flow state? By engaging with all of these attributes in meaningful conversation.

Easier said than done, trust me.

Flow won't happen in every interaction. In fact, it may show up in just one conversation a day. But the goal is to try. To reach for it. To let these attributes flow through your words, your presence, your energy.

It's incredible how much can transform when those flow-state conversations occur.

Hopefully, you'll begin to experience this flow state both personally and professionally throughout your day. The ultimate goal is to tap into that state during all your conversations. Connecting across different personalities, gender gaps, and varying perspectives can be challenging. But after reading this book, you'll gain a better understanding of how to navigate those interactions with greater ease and confidence.

By developing your personal attributes and crafting your own Core CARE Equation, there's no reason you can't engage all twelve components to make your interactions more positive and meaningful.

This book is centered on personal growth as the foundation for professional success and organizational strength. This starts with leadership, how we view it, use it, and how impactful being authentic and relatable are. In turn, this fuels cultural development and, most importantly, human improvement. Yes, we're talking EQ!

So, how do you take great conversations and make them even better? By using the CARE Framework to explore and explain how to unlock the elusive "IT Factor."

What's the "IT Factor"? I hear you asking. "What is flow state? What kind of book is this?!"

Trust me, it'll all make sense. When your head and heart are fully aligned in the present moment (even just briefly), that is the *IT Factor*.

It doesn't happen all the time, and sometimes it flashes like lightning—there one moment, gone the next. But what if there were a way to make that flash last longer?

That's what this book is designed to help you do.

It's about being vulnerable. It's about acknowledging the struggles we all face. Greatness isn't about chasing perfection; it's about learning through failure. When your head and heart are disconnected, that's often when mistakes happen. Each chapter combines a personal story or real-life struggle with a professional lesson. It's the beauty of perfect imperfection. It's about harnessing the power of the flow state to build lasting relationships.

This book is generationally transferable: its insights are relevant across times and ages. And one thing's for sure: **This book will not be negative**.

It's self-improvement on a positive scale. Life doesn't automatically deflect the bad, but you can learn how to navigate it better.

CHAPTER 1

It All Starts With Consistency!

IN MY TWELVE-ATTRIBUTE SYSTEM, consistency is arguably the most important trait. In fact, you can place the word "consistently" in front of every other attribute I'll discuss, and it fits. You can be consistently compassionate, consistently curious, and consistently relatable.

Later in the book, this attribute will echo throughout the chapters, amplifying the impact of the others, almost like giving them superpowers, simply because consistency is applied to your daily grind. Consistency is truly the fuel that powers the engine when you're building a personality that attracts others, makes them want to be around you, and inspires them to learn from you.

It is crucial to understand the significance of consistency. While many people talk about the importance of being consistent, they often struggle with how to put it into practice. To make it easier, I've broken consistency down into manageable steps. Each day, set three goals: one self-goal, one personal goal, and one professional goal.

Everyone's routine will look different, and that's okay. For me, separating goals into the categories of self, personal, and professional works well. Others may find alternative systems that better suit their lifestyles, and that's perfectly fine too.

Starting with the "self," it's important to prioritize your well-being. This means waking up early to work out and taking care of your body. By "self," I'm referring to what you consume. Hydration is essential, so drink plenty of water, and make sure to include protein in your diet. This book will touch on health topics because I've made significant lifestyle changes related to health and fitness.

Once you've taken care of yourself and completed your workout, it's time to focus on the "personal" aspect. I like to call my mom on my way to work, whether I'm driving or commuting by train. This helps me stay connected and nurture those important relationships.

Finally, there's the "professional" side. You can often integrate personal and self-care tasks while planning your day. If you anticipate a productive day, consider setting three goals, but be mindful not to overextend yourself. Leaving the day with unmet goals can be discouraging. Remember, there's always tomorrow to catch up. Accomplishing three well-chosen goals makes for a great day. It's a fact: achieving these goals consistently allows you to take on more. Consistency creates space in your schedule, boosts your mindset, and gives you more time back. In other words, consistency yields an ROT: a return on time!

It's crucial to avoid taking on too much at once. I've seen many people become overwhelmed and unbalanced. Start with one goal for self, one for personal, and one for professional. If you feel comfortable adding more, go for it, but always do what works best for you.

As you form this habit consistently over time, people will begin to recognize you for it. They'll know that you have a self-goal, a personal goal, and a professional goal. Eventually, you may expand this list and start aiming for two or even three self-goals. I found it amusing when I first started this practice. I'd often complete my personal goals by noon, which made me realize that I needed to space them out throughout the day. Now, I typically place my personal goal at the end of the day and my professional goal in the middle, aligning more naturally with when most people are working.

It's one thing to talk about being consistent, but it's another to actually live it. At forty years old, I struggled with consistency. While I was successfully growing a business and thriving professionally, I wasn't consistent with my personal priorities. At the time, I weighed seventy pounds more than I do now at fifty. I was also battling an addiction to tobacco, which (thankfully) I overcame that same year. By the time I was forty-five, I recognized the need to quit alcohol. Although I have a slight allergy to it, I was a binge drinker. One drink, two... or why not five or six, right? Wrong. I needed to change. I just needed the right push at the right time.

My focus shifted to longevity, and I began to see it as critical that I stay consistent in being true to myself. Between the ages of forty and fifty, I lost sixty-five pounds, and I've kept it off. I came to understand that consistency was key to my well-being. It didn't take any external push; I simply realized that my old habits no longer served me, and I took pride in making the decision to change. That consistent effort has truly added years to my life.

People often ask me, "Jonathan, why did you make those changes?" The answer is twofold: first, I want to ensure my longevity on this planet, and second, I want to be there for my kids for as long as possible. I also want my wife to have me around for the long haul. If I were to break the good habits I've built, I'd be cheating myself, and that's something I wanted to eliminate from the beginning.

One important point I want to emphasize is the value of simple things, like being on time. I've always been taught that being fifteen minutes early is on time. Punctuality matters. It shows respect, as I'll explore more deeply later in the book.

Consistency in behavior is key, and I've found journaling to be a powerful tool in this area. It helps me maintain clarity in my thoughts and stay grounded. As a fifty-year-old man who has experienced both highs and lows and has helped build a business from the ground up, writing things down has become a steady habit that supports my personal growth.

Let me be clear: I'm not perfect, and I never will be. I'm still working on many aspects of my life. The goal of this book is to help you understand that if you follow this framework, you can improve: not necessarily become perfect, but simply become better. This commitment to self-improvement can take you as far as you're willing to go.

Now, let's talk about inconsistency. Inconsistent behavior can lead to a breakdown in reliability, both personally and professionally. When friends or colleagues can't count on you, when you say you'll show up and don't, or when communication is lacking, it creates uncertainty. People don't know what to expect, and that undermines trust. Consistency and execution go hand in hand: you can't execute well without consistency, and you won't maintain consistency without execution.

Many people have asked me how to break bad habits. For me, envisioning my life and thinking about my kids played a crucial role in quitting tobacco, to which I was addicted. I pictured my kids standing over my coffin, asking why I never quit, wondering why that habit was more important than them. That moment defined my decision to stop using tobacco, and that was it.

Similarly, a friend once challenged me to a thirty-day no-drinking challenge. I realized that even if I had a good time that night, I'd wake up the next morning ready to walk away from alcohol for good. I knew my tendency to binge drink: if I had one drink, I'd end up having six or seven. That wasn't the person I wanted to be. I thought about how alcohol could damage my health and potentially take away the years I had fought so hard to reclaim. So, I made the decision to eliminate it from my life. That was nearly five years ago. Now, I don't even think about it. Sobriety is simply a consistent part of who I am, and I talk about it openly in the hope that it might help others.

You cannot be a toe dipper. What's a toe dipper? Exactly what it sounds like. You know the type: the person who walks around the edge of the pool and just dips their toes in, thinking the water might be too cold, instead of just jumping into the damn water.

You can spot a toe dipper from a mile away. The people who say they're going to be there, but they really aren't. The people who say they're going to read up on your company, but they don't. And then when they show up, they're clueless as to what your vision for the company is. Those are the toe-dippers, doing "just enough," but you can't fool the focused. They'll see right through you. Consistency is a must for personal and professional growth.

Every day is an interview. That's right, you're interviewing today: are you ready? Treating every day like an interview is a mindset that I have focused on throughout my career. Think about consistency as an attribute, and apply the mindset that you're interviewing every day. I bet you're early for that interview. I bet you're dressed for success, you've done all your homework, and you're ready to crush it! Why not apply that same mentality to every day you live? Think about it: it makes sense and ensures that you're remembered for all the right reasons.

Another mindset that helps with consistency, especially in leadership, is the idea to "Always Be Teaching" (ABT). Whether I was in Detroit in the early days of 2000, helping the Eight Eleven Group grow our first satellite market, or when I had moved to Philadelphia to get that market going, I always taught what I was doing in the moment. Before the Detroit market, I had never built a business up from scratch, so I was learning on the job. I wanted everyone to learn on the fly with me. So, it was imperative to take the time to explain the reason behind my actions. Even more so, it had to be a consistent habit.

It became a syllabus within a day, not just a syllabus they were going to take and shove into their desk and never use. I wanted them to know everything

I was doing every time I took an action. So, if I were going to email a client, I would tell them *why* I was emailing the client. I got specific, painting a picture of the *why* behind my action. If I were going to a new meeting, I would take them with me. If I was going to go down in a ball of fire, they needed to see how I'd handle it. They needed to see an authentic sales approach. If I were going to call a manager, or if there was a reason why I was approaching a client in a certain way, I wanted my team to understand that reasoning (ABT!). There was a reason for it.

It became almost like the teaching hospitals in America, where I created teaching environments within the company and markets I helped build. I wanted everybody to be learning. So, leaders out there, please don't ever stop teaching: always be teaching, always transferring knowledge in the moment, and frankly, answering their *why* before they have a chance to ask it.

Why did I do this? I was building a business. My team needed to know everything. Building a business is like going to war. You need a team that understands the fight, and that it will take all of us to seize each day.

Your managers will see it. One piece of advice for all of you: always be standing in a lobby. Ryan Hasbrook, my first professional boss and, to this day, my great friend, taught me to always be standing in a lobby, never sitting. That developed into a consistent habit that I continue to teach. When you're sitting, it can appear as though you're not ready or not engaged in the moment. That posture can be perceived as laziness, even if that's not the case. Therefore, avoid sitting in a lobby, unless you're at a doctor's office or specifically instructed to do so.

Consistency was also crucial in my experience as a former chief experience officer (CXO) for the Eight Eleven Group. Everything about experience revolves around consistency. It's about how you make people feel after you've left. To build solid relationships that can evolve into true partnerships, the experience must remain consistent. The figure below illustrates the steps toward developing true partnerships.

If a significant client moves to another company, they'll likely bring you with them. This happens because you've established consistent habits in your interactions. The experiences you've delivered have been uniform throughout.

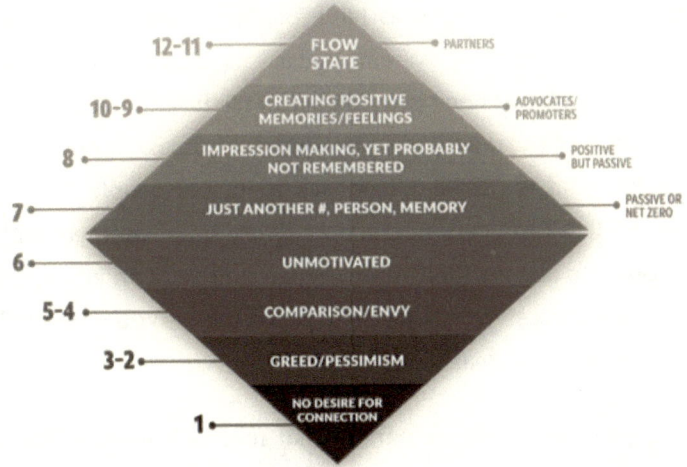

You cannot afford to be inconsistent in how you treat clients or interact with coworkers. Consistency is essential. Your attitude shapes everything. How you present yourself is critical to how others perceive you. If your attitudes fluctuate due to personal circumstances and you bring that inconsistency into the workplace, it can negatively impact how you are viewed.

That's why I previously mentioned the importance of setting a personal goal to accomplish before work. This helps you feel good about yourself, maintain a positive outlook, and acknowledge that you've already achieved something that day. Then, focus on your professional goals with a great attitude, because each day is essentially an interview. Wrap up your day with a personal goal, whether it's taking your wife to dinner or playing catch with your kids. That's a fulfilling day.

A positive attitude and consistent habits lead to great experiences for others. This is essential for building partnerships. I've managed to maintain relationships with clients who would greet me warmly if we met today, demonstrating the value of these connections.

Building balance, consistent patterns, and feedback loops are also crucial in this context. Many industries lack sufficient feedback. Surveys can certainly be helpful, and many companies have platforms for gathering responses. We're all familiar with rating systems that ask us to score various experiences. These can be useful, but none provide better feedback than direct, in-person communication with managers, coworkers, bosses, family, or friends. Therefore, it's vital to create a feedback loop. Let people know you'll be requesting feedback in every interaction. Every time you meet with a client, make it a point to ask for their input. When you send an email, ensure that your message was received as intended. When you leave a voicemail, confirm that your message was clearly understood.

Everything you do should be part of that feedback loop, allowing you to gauge how those around you feel about their interactions with you. Establishing balance, consistency, and feedback loops can help you determine whether you've effectively engaged with a client or identify areas needing improvement, whether in your professional life or personal interactions, such as communicating differently with your children based on age differences.

Once again, in discussing consistency, consider whether you're consistently communicating both verbally and nonverbally. If you say you're going to email someone at two o'clock and it doesn't arrive until 2:04, that's inconsistent. Your reliability suffers, and as a result, you may lose business.

If you write a letter that never gets sent, that's a significant issue. When you're sitting in front of a client and not paying attention, you're sending signals that imply inconsistency in your behavior and attitude, which can damage your relationships.

Are you showing up on time? Are you keeping your promises? It's time to take action.

The small things add up to red flags, and your clients notice them the moment you walk in the door. This book isn't about marketing materials; it's about how to be a better human in front of your clients. Bringing a consistent attitude to your personal and professional interactions can set the tone for achieving your desired outcomes.

Throughout this book, I'll discuss the **Core CARE Equation**. There is a corporate Core CARE Equation and an industry Core CARE Equation that every company could display on their website, and frankly, they should. I'll cover each of these equations as we progress through the book.

Perhaps it's a coincidence, but consistency is the first element I've always included in my CARE Framework, and it's the top attribute for the corporate Core CARE Equation. In a corporate environment, if you lack consistency, your brand and company will not grow. Consistency is the number one attribute that clients seek in you, your company, or the products they are considering purchasing.

Consider examples like Chick-fil-A, In-N-Out Burger, or Culver's (if they are available in your area), or how the staff at Nordstrom treats you when you enter the store. Brands like Starbucks consistently write messages on their cups, claiming to provide a uniform drink experience. While my drink may not always be made the same way, they are willing to remake it for you, which shows their commitment to consistency.

This consistent attitude and presentation are what keep their brand thriving and encourage customers to return. It's why people often remark that they forgot Chick-fil-A is closed on Sundays. When people are so engaged with a brand that they forget it's closed on certain days, you know you have a strong and growing brand.

Inconsistent behaviors ultimately lead to cheating yourself and your brand. Just like people become known for specific traits or sayings, you can develop a reputation based on your actions. For instance, I used to greet everyone by saying, "What's going on, Philly? How are we doing today?" People recognized that as my signature greeting, which created a sense of reliability around my attitude.

When you're consistent, people can depend on you. If you're inconsistent, it can leave your team wondering what's wrong with you. Thus, it's vital to maintain a positive demeanor. Once you've established a pattern, there's no reason to break it. In fact, when you're inconsistent, you undermine your own potential.

This concept applies in various aspects of life. For example, while working out or dieting, having cheat days is acceptable; perfection is not the goal. Greatness isn't about always being perfect. Rather, it's about minimizing inconsistencies.

Let me share a story from my early days in Detroit. I was very strict about punctuality. If it was 8:01 a.m. and you weren't at your desk, I had no problem sending you home. I would drive forty-five minutes to work and arrive half an hour early, while some new hires, who lived just a few minutes away, would roll in at 8:04 or 8:05 a.m. after partying the night before. I saw their tardiness as disrespectful, so I would simply ask them to come back the next day.

I believe that if you want to build your dreams, you have to show commitment. I thought teaching them how to be more consistent meant punishing them, instead of explaining why showing up at 8:04 or 8:05 was really just allowing a lack of consistency to occur. That was no way to grow a business. So leaders reading this, make sure you keep a "teach first" environment.

Inconsistent behavior not only undermines reliability but can also erode trust. If you exhibit inconsistent patterns, your team won't trust you. This is why a leader with high EQ might advise you to stay home if you know you can't bring your "A" game. Bringing negativity into the workplace only harms productivity.

Inconsistent behaviors cheat you and tarnish your brand. This is why companies often encourage employees to take breaks, go for a walk, or work out during lunch. They aim to relieve stress and maintain consistency in behaviors.

Moreover, inconsistency raises red flags. For example, if I'm reviewing a résumé and I see gaps in employment or frequent job changes, like a couple of years in one place followed by several months off, these inconsistent patterns stand out as potential concerns. When you apply for credit at a bank, the longer you've been employed at a company, the more credit you're typically allowed to receive, as it demonstrates a consistent work history. This principle not only applies to what I'm focusing on in this book, but it's also essential for securing loans in life!

The cost of being inconsistent is looking around and seeing no one there to support you. It's realizing that no one is writing you a thank-you note or wondering where your clients have gone.

Inconsistency could even be a factor in why you might be single, or it may contribute to being unhealthy. There's a measure of consistency that can truly impact your life if you don't pay attention to it. For instance, people with high blood pressure need to be consistent in monitoring their diet. I have diabetes in my family history, and dementia also runs in my family. So, being mentally sharp is very important. There's a cost to inconsistent behavior—it can lead to you falling off track.

I've made the commitment to never consume tobacco or alcohol again. However, not everyone has that same level of resolve. Inconsistent behavior can bring you closer to dangerous situations, and I won't let that happen to me.

When people are inconsistent, they often feel off balance. That's okay, but it's crucial to keep those inconsistencies from influencing your brand or your image.

I was once addicted to tobacco and struggled with alcohol. Since I began writing this book, many people have mentioned that the section about alcohol might be one of the most crucial parts of the book. There are countless individuals out there who just can't seem to grasp that part of their lives.

I don't intend for this to be a self-help book, nor do I think I'm better than anyone else. But let me be clear: this is not just about my book; this is serious. This is critical for understanding how long you want to live. There's a saying people often use: "I would die for my wife or my children." Honestly, I hope that's not the case. What I want is for you to want to live for your children, live for your spouse, and cherish those memories.

Inconsistent behaviors can lead to inconsistent choices, which often result in catastrophes. Therefore, maintaining balance in your consistency is essential.

How are you showing up? It's important to reflect on this. We should ask ourselves, *How am I showing up?* Think about how some classic characters enter a room—like Norm from *Cheers*, or Kramer from *Seinfeld*.

Personally and professionally, consistency is a must. Whether you're growing yourself or your career, if you take a big swig of consistency every morning, you're growing both. Action is everything. Take action on being consistent personally with daily goals. Take action on being consistent professionally by how you show up! Stay consistent. Check the attitude at the door! You and the people you come in contact with deserve the best version of yourself, and that best version starts with consistency.

CHAPTER 2

Do People Really Know How Much You Care?

COMPASSION IS THE SECOND attribute in my CARE Framework, and is critical for building authentic connections and lasting relationships. It's essential when trying to simply relate to others. In this chapter, I explore the most challenging parts of my life that have become the foundation for the person I have evolved into today. You have your own life experiences and challenges that have shaped your ability to connect with deeper compassion (or will shape it in the future). It is in these life experiences that your compassion can lead the way.

As you read, think about your experiences and how they have shaped you. The world is filled with pain, struggle, loss, and love. Be willing to listen to others. It can be where some of your most lasting relationships come from.

To begin, I want to clarify the three levels of compassion:

1. **Stranger Compassion:** Holding the door for a mother struggling with a toddler in tow, or stopping to help a family with a flat tire.

2. **Familiar Compassion:** This comes into play when you have a relationship with someone you recognize or know, perhaps a friend or a coworker.

3. **Family Compassion:** This should be the deepest, as it involves those you love most, your family and close friends. It is also the most challenging due to complicated family histories and emotions.

While family compassion is significant, we'll focus mostly on stranger and familiar compassion, as we encounter these types daily. Often, the compassion we show to strangers can evolve into familiar compassion. The moment you make eye contact or introduce yourself, you transition from a stranger to someone familiar.

Starting your day with the mindset of carrying a smile into every room you walk into is one of the most effective ways to lead with compassion. It lets the room know you're approachable, and that goes hand in hand with compassion. This simple act can convey kindness when meeting someone new.

Familiar compassion arises when a friend or someone close to you faces hardship. You want to be there for them at a funeral, during surgery, or at a court hearing, for example.

Now, why is compassion so important? Compassion allows you to see past the title, whether it be friend, neighbor, or CEO, to connect with the person. Regardless of where you are personally or professionally, we have all had a journey. No one's path is without challenges, and it is compassion for one another's struggles that leads to authentic connections.

I have struggled with my own experiences of tragedy and loss, which have only amplified my level of compassion. One day in particular changed my life irrevocably. On August 3, 1999, at approximately 2:20 in the afternoon, I lost my brother, Rob. He was twenty-eight years old and had four children under the age of ten. He was the source of my ambition, drive, and enthusiasm for life. He was one of my older brothers—the one most similar to me—and my best friend. Tragically, he passed away in front of me due to liver failure.

Telling four children that their dad was no longer sick put everything into perspective for me. This experience shaped how I approach hiring people in my professional life. I always hold a place in my heart for those who have faced struggles, be it divorce, cancer, health issues, or loss.

Recently, I believed my father was simply slowing down with age. In truth, he was suffering from late-stage Lewy body dementia, a disease few people understand. It is one of the most devastating conditions, as it affects the brain's ability to discern what is real and what is not; ultimately, you no longer recognize the people around you.

Losing my father and witnessing his transition from life to death has deepened my desire to understand others' struggles. These experiences happen in real life, and they matter.

Compassion is essential. There's nothing more important in this world than offering compassion to someone in need, whether that means providing advice or simply lending an ear.

Are you the one who can be there for them? Will you ask a curious question or be a shoulder to cry on? I'm still processing the loss of my brother, which happened twenty-five years ago, and my father's passing just a few years back. While my dad's death was challenging, hospice care provided peace; the tragedy of my brother's loss feels even more profound.

Rob loved U2. He went to over six concerts to see them play. Following his lead, I fell in love with them too, and I found some sense of healing through their music. Rob loved the album, *The Joshua Tree,* the most, so I chose to honor him with a tattoo of a Joshua Tree on the top of my left shoulder. I cried the entire time, not from the pain of the needle but from the pain of missing him. One tattoo became a collection on my upper left arm, each one honoring my brother. Through fate or perhaps something higher, just a few years ago my brother's widow and kids met Bono briefly before U2's *Joshua Tree* tour stop in Detroit. Bono remembered meeting Missy and a couple of my brother's kids before the show. Then, in true world-class fashion, Bono dedicated "One Tree Hill" to Rob. True story—just search U2 *One Tree Hill Ford Field*.

So when my dad passed, it was a no-brainer that I needed to honor him as well. He was a great man who taught me the value of hard work from a young age. I designed another tattoo to honor him and his legacy of raising four boys with the values of hard work and a strong sense of family.

When I interact with people outside of work, I connect with their stories because loss is a universal experience. I once thought I was immune to death until I witnessed my brother's passing and had to tell his four children that their dad was no longer sick, but also that he wouldn't be coming home.

Showing compassion is essential not just as a family value, but as a fundamental human experience.

As I share this, perhaps it resonates with you. Maybe you can relate, or perhaps you're going through a similar situation right now. You're not alone. For me, this experience became a source of strength, something that makes me unique.

Compassion can be expressed in various ways. You might offer a hug, tilt your head in understanding, or simply communicate through your voice. Writing a heartfelt letter, planning a special day for someone, or forwarding an encouraging message to provide support: these are all acts of compassion.

When was the last time someone reached out to you just to check in? A simple "How are you? Are you hanging in there?" can mean so much.

How do you carry compassion? You carry it by recognizing that you never truly know why someone is not smiling. You can't see the struggles behind their frown or what lies beyond their smile. Extend that understanding when someone shares their story of loss, be it a father, brother, or another loved one, or even going through a divorce. I've walked through many of these hardships, and I've transformed them into strengths.

My brother is with me every day. He was there with me in Philadelphia, in Detroit, when I married my wonderful wife, Danielle, and when my children were born. He accompanies me in everything I do. I still talk to him; he remains my best friend.

When you encounter difficult situations in life, don't push them aside. It's important to acknowledge them rather than bury them under a rug. Pain is a burden that is lighter when shared. While I understand not everyone feels comfortable sharing their experiences as I do, there are many like me who are willing to listen, offer support, and understand your pain.

The first day I woke up without my dad was strange, a surreal moment when I realized that the one man who had always been there for me was no longer present. If you haven't experienced this kind of loss, cherish the moments you have with your dad. Hug him.

Compassion is key to building lasting relationships. When it comes to professional interactions, showing compassion toward your client base is crucial. The moment you meet a client, you begin to establish familiarity.

If a client shares a story with you, set aside your pen and paper. Don't focus on your brochure or your wallet, just listen to them. When a client opens up with a compassionate tone, you've already begun to break down barriers. Shift your mindset from being just a salesperson to someone who is there to listen and support. Remember that everyone is dealing with their own challenges.

Early in my professional career, I worked for a staffing firm in Grand Rapids, MI. I would drive from Grand Rapids to Fremont, MI, where my client's headquarters were located. There, I met a manager who was battling breast cancer at the time. I had just lost my brother, it was worth the 2 hour drive to see her as she became like a mother figure to me. I could go into her office, close the door, and talk about my brother while she talked to me about her fight against cancer. I remember celebrating milestones with her as she reached one year, then two years, cancer-free.

The relationship we built was powerful. A few years later, I found myself as one of the primary vendors within that client, handling various operational needs. This happened not because I was trying to sell them something, but because I was there seeking emotional support as a twenty-four-year-old struggling with loss. I just drove there to talk to someone who would listen, and that's what compassion is all about: helping each other through difficult times. Understanding that everyone deals with personal struggles can be a strength. If you're a salesperson solely focused on making money, your clients will sense it, and that insincerity can be disheartening.

Being genuine is an essential part of compassion. If you can't show compassion to the people you're trying to build relationships with, you'll never succeed. Building connections is similar to dating. If every interaction feels like an interview, then showing compassion during those moments becomes even more important.

It's also essential to read the room and engage meaningfully. These interactions are not just transactions. Approach them with a relational mindset. When someone opens up to you, put down your pen, tilt your head, and empathize with their situation. Listen actively; these moments are about nurturing relationships, not just business.

As you work to turn a stranger's need for compassion into a familiar connection, remember to listen and be present. If they cry, offer a tissue. At the end of your conversation, give them a handshake and, if appropriate, a gentle hug. When a manager opens up and shares their stories with you, listen. Be receptive to their experiences and the challenges they face, not just focused on how to fill your wallet. Everyone has their own issues, and showing compassion can make a significant difference. Clients are not just people looking to hand you millions of dollars with every project. Everyone faces their own challenges.

I find it difficult to talk about my brother and my dad, but I want the world to know that it is possible to overcome loss, apply those experiences to your story, and have people support you. That's exactly what I did.

When my brother passed away, I faced a fork in the road. I could have chosen a destructive path and likely wouldn't have been around much longer. Instead, I decided to leave Battle Creek, Michigan, and pursue my dreams.

I have stayed connected with Missy and my brother's children, and to this day, they know they can reach out to me for support or advice. That connection is truly beautiful. Recently, I was a groomsman at one of their weddings, and I felt proud. But first, I had to go find myself, discover my purpose, and carve my own path.

When I moved to Philadelphia, many of my relationships were built around compassion because I didn't have any friends or clients there. Utilizing my twelve attributes allowed me to build a thriving East Coast market and create lifelong, lasting relationships. Thankfully, I can proudly say that the Eight Eleven Group still has a few clients from that time.

When you care, compassion becomes a familiar response. You love your partner, and that love forms the foundation of your compassion. You don't have to experience the same situation to understand that. While you may not fully grasp what they're going through, you can still be present for them. You can be there to support your partner. You're the one initiating the outreach.

Even if you haven't gone through a similar experience, reaching out with compassion is essential. If you look deeper into your own life, you'll likely find someone in your family whom you can call who has faced a similar challenge. You're just one call away from someone who has felt it.

Thank goodness you haven't experienced that loss yourself, but you don't need to have gone through it to empathize. You simply need to feel it.

When clients come to me and share their stories, I truly feel their pain. It doesn't matter what I'm offering; they're not just buying a product, they're seeking authenticity and connection with me.

I've encountered many people in my life, and I don't shy away from hiring those who haven't faced significant challenges themselves. Instead, I want to understand how they've helped others. What have they done to support someone in need?

Do you need to have experienced loss to write a heartfelt letter? The answer is no. You can make a day special for your partner and help them feel better without having encountered loss. For example, you might hear a message on a podcast that resonates with you and think, *This could help him/her.* You can simply forward that message to them. Random acts of kindness can reflect a compassionate demeanor.

It's genuine to empathize and support someone, even without having experienced the same pain. Remember, everyone has pain, but not everyone wants to share it. If you're blessed to be called upon to be the listener, it's an honor you shouldn't take lightly. When my nephews or nieces call me, I will stop whatever I am doing to be there for them. I know somewhere, Rob smiles every time I'm there for them.

Every time I stop at a red light and see someone holding out money or a sign, I feel compelled to give them everything in my wallet. Often, traffic is moving, and I can't, but there's a story behind each of those individuals. Every single one of them has a unique story, and I can't help but think about it.

My mom and dad raised us to show everyone respect. People who are struggling deserve our respect and compassion. How could their circumstances have benefited from basic compassion? They find themselves in terrible situations, and no one truly knows their lives. No one needs to endure the hardships I faced to show compassion. That should already be a part of us.

I've had many clients ask to meet with me, and when I arrive, it often has nothing to do with business. They just want my company, and I love that. It gives me a sense of pride. They reach out to me not solely based on what I'm selling, but because they know my relationship is genuine. They've heard my story and know they can confide in me. They know I'll understand their pain or problem. That's a great level in a relationship to aspire to get to. If your clients don't ever open up, don't let you in, it might not be them. It may be in how you walk in the door.

Compassion personally strengthens relationships, and professionally lays the groundwork that can lead to lasting personal connections with business partners. "Meetings" turn into something more when you have built a relationship beyond the "transaction."

CHAPTER 3

Curiosity, It's About Building Trust!

CURIOSITY IS IMPORTANT because it shows genuine interest and a desire to connect with someone on a deeper level. I believe curiosity gained significance in my life during my early twenties, when I realized I had come from a small town, attended a small school, and that the world was a vast place.

I grew up in Battle Creek, Michigan, and attended St. Phillip Catholic High School. I graduated with just thirty-eight classmates and then moved on to Central Michigan University (CMU). The experience of going from a class of thirty-eight to a student body of 16,000 expanded my world dramatically. Even something as simple as the dress code, which allowed me to wear jeans, fueled my curiosity during that time. While classroom curiosity is key, having a larger lens on life can perhaps give you an equally important vantage point of learning and perspective. Professors may not want to hear that, but it's true. Curiosity is key to gaining knowledge and understanding opposing views. It's also how you build relationships based on trust and reliability.

Hey leaders out there, listen up....curiosity isn't just about asking questions; it's about building trust and respect. When you demonstrate curiosity, such as by asking follow-up questions, people notice. They realize you're genuinely interested in what they have to say, which opens up the conversation. Curiosity fosters connection.

CFO Jeff Weiser, my friend and co-founder of the Eight Eleven Group, exemplifies this trait. He is one of the most curious people I know. Jeff has a genuine desire to ask questions, not because he doesn't know the answers, but because he truly wants to understand your answers. He's always seeking to understand the thought processes of others.

This is the basic principle of "practice what you preach." When you engage with people and ask questions, you show respect, and with every inquiry, you strengthen rapport. It's vital to keep asking follow-up questions until you've thoroughly explored a topic. That's what curiosity is all about. When you genuinely engage like this, you inevitably get to know the person on a deeper level. I learned that by watching Jeff asking, not just for an answer, but to build an understanding.

At the beginning of my career, I'll admit that curiosity was one of my weaker traits. I was cautious when engaging with new clients. I didn't always have a natural inclination to be curious professionally. Fortunately, I had a colleague and mentor, Ryan Hasbrook (CEO and co-founder of the Eight Eleven Group), who helped me recognize the importance of this attribute. He had a unique way of tilting his head and asking open-ended questions like, "Can you help me understand that better?" This approach not only encouraged others to share more, but also created a deeper connection.

Ultimately, his method wasn't just about learning. It was about building trust, connection, and synergy. Curiosity acts as the binder that strengthens relationships. If you become known for being curious, you'll be recognized as someone eager to learn and willing to go the extra mile.

Curiosity isn't just about asking questions; it's about building trust and respect. In a professional context, when we talk about curiosity, it's essential to ask secondary questions. You've probably heard this in countless business books: never ask closed-ended questions to a client, as you won't gain any valuable insight. Instead, focus on asking open-ended follow-up questions to keep the dialogue flowing. When clients share their thoughts, remember that it might not align with your preconceived notions about the direction of the meeting. It doesn't always go as planned. Asking secondary questions is the best way to stand out from your competition and foster trust.

This process might lead you down a personal rabbit hole, but it's worthwhile to let the client steer the conversation instead of trying to control it yourself. At the end of every client interaction, it's extremely important to establish a "feedback loop." I briefly touched on this earlier in the book, but a feedback loop is simply the conscious effort of checking in with your client and asking for feedback in real time. You always want to know how you're doing and aim to establish a feedback loop after every interaction. That's being curious.

If you're reading this and realize you didn't ask for feedback after your last interaction, then we've just identified an area of opportunity. It's actually quite simple. At the end of a meeting, ask the manager, client, or coworker:

- "Was there anything you were confused about or anything that raised an eyebrow?"

- "Is there anything you plan to discuss at dinner tonight?"

- "I want to ensure I've addressed all your questions before leaving."

Again, be curious, not just fulfilling a KPI.

- "I'll be upfront: I'm going to ask you for feedback every time we meet. I aim to create a consistent feedback loop centered on curiosity."

This approach allows you to build a professional relationship grounded in transparency and reinforces that your curiosity comes from a place of better serving your client's needs.

By creating a feedback loop, you also communicate the *why* behind your actions. Respect grows when you establish this loop with coworkers, bosses, clients, family members, and friends. This is both a personal and professional discipline. When working with a confused coworker, their feedback can help clarify your message or improve their understanding before you conclude the conversation. Asking your partner what they did or didn't like about the new restaurant you tried last weekend allows you to better understand what restaurants to try in the future. It's a small gesture that can yield big insight.

I've mentioned earlier how experiences shape our emotions. Asking, "How did that make you feel?" is critical. Everyone in the service industry or anyone selling a product (so essentially, everyone) should actively seek feedback in real time. If you don't, you're missing out on opportunities to gain a deeper level of understanding.

Every time you leave a meeting, you have a chance to receive feedback. Whether it's positive or critical, all feedback is valuable. When you consistently ask for feedback, it demonstrates your commitment to improvement. I often ask my clients why they choose to work with me. Their responses usually highlight my eagerness, enthusiasm, and consistent request for feedback, indicating a desire for growth.

Remember, a brochure might explain the product, but the feedback loop you cultivate is vital for establishing lasting partnerships. Approach every interaction with genuine curiosity and provide a clear explanation of your intentions. This has to be amplified as a leader! Creating the feedback loop with your people creates an environment where they don't feel like they're being judged. Rather, they're thrilled that there's a leader out there who really cares how they're feeling and wants to know how they can improve… powerful leadership.

It's important for your clients to understand from the start that you'll be asking questions. For a long time, even within the Eight Eleven Group, I invested in a product designed to help us send out surveys after the completion of a project. While sending these surveys is beneficial, if you aren't asking your clients about their experience in real time, while sitting face-to-face with them, then you're missing out on the opportunity for true human connection.

Don't hesitate to ask for feedback in the moment. Every salesperson reading this should ask for feedback at the end of their next meeting. Period.

This is something I'm passionate about. There's nothing worse than returning to your office and saying, "Yeah, it was a great meeting," and when asked about follow-up, responding, "We were going to set that up." Well, why didn't you set it up while you were there? That feedback loop should have included scheduling the next steps. If you don't, you risk losing valuable opportunities.

A good tactical plan that leverages curiosity to build client and organizational knowledge can help you stand out as a knowledgeable resource rather than just a vendor. This approach helped me rise to the top of many vendor lists.

I have my own professional example of this with a large Fortune 50 client we targeted. When I was in Philadelphia, this company was our biggest prospect, with around 180,000 employees, many of them working in IT. I told my sales team, which consisted of three people at the time, that we would not be asking for business until the timing was right. We needed to learn enough about their technical environment so we could handle any projects they presented to us. The company was in hypergrowth and was cutting-edge, and they didn't just throw requirements your way. If you weren't qualified, you would be dismissed and lose your chance for future work.

For a year and a half, we engaged with this client, holding meetings, lunches, and happy hours, without ever asking for business. We focused on learning about their environment. Curiosity was key. Finally, the right opportunity arose, and the consistent curiosity paid off. One of their long-standing vendors had become complacent, and our Fortune 50 target was ready to give us a chance. They understood that we had the knowledge needed to take on the work.

With the help of my colleagues, Jordan Strozza, Rachel Morrison, Bobby Bauscher, Stephanie White, and others from my Philadelphia office, we succeeded in securing this Fortune 50 giant as a client. For over a year and a half, we achieved this without ever asking for business. We approached every interaction with them as an opportunity to gain knowledge and establish ourselves as a trusted partner.

For every salesperson out there listening or reading this: stop focusing solely on closing the deal today. Start thinking about learning today for potential business tomorrow. Curiosity can take you from there.

The Cost of a Lack of Curiosity

Ineptitude often feels like embarking on a quest for treasure without a map. It's nearly impossible to set a navigational course in your life without curiosity as a key. Moreover, curiosity allows people to see that you're in the room and that you're present.

How will you know whether to go left or right without asking questions and understanding what options are available? A person lacking curiosity lacks direction. When you don't have a follow-up question, you're showing a lack of interest. And if you're not interested in the person in front of you, why would they be invested in you or your success in return?

Being curious when you engage in conversation can encourage others to open up and share more. Oftentimes, people perceive curiosity as a weakness and avoid asking questions in group settings because of it. But in reality, those who ask questions are often the brightest in the room.

The impact of using a curious approach to breaking into the Fortune 50 was profound. That opportunity helped shape the future of the Philadelphia market and the employees who worked within it.

The cost of complacency is that you can't expect to be at the front of the line. Reliability diminishes, and you end up living in a shallow bubble, unaware of what's happening in your field and in society more broadly. This is one of the negative consequences we face as a country. We seem unwilling to understand each other. Isn't it better to see first and understand subsequently? That's the essence of curiosity. It's what Dale Carnegie taught us in his book, *How to Win Friends and Influence People*: *"Instead of condemning people, let's try to understand them."* So why don't we practice this more as humans?

As a person, I acknowledge that I tend to be very defensive. However, using curiosity helps me break down that barrier. When my wife says something that might trigger my defensiveness, I push myself to ask a follow-up question like, "What did you mean by that?" rather than jumping to my own conclusion about the thought behind her statement. This approach allows me to reframe my reactions. Without that curiosity, I would be missing the opportunity to better understand the feelings of my partner.

I find that embracing curiosity helps me work through many of my little "pet peeves." Slow drivers used to frustrate me incredibly, but instead of reacting with anger, I now try to cultivate curiosity. I wonder what might be going on with the slow driver. Are they a student driver? My son will be learning to drive soon. Are they older? Are they experiencing a medical issue? Maybe that's just their speed, and I need to enjoy the ride.

Embracing curiosity helps lower my temper and makes me more accepting of the situation. It is what it is; they are driving slowly. In this way, curiosity can serve as a thermostat in your life when applied correctly.

This highlights something I've mentioned before: it's not really about asking questions. It's more about trust and the importance of building, strengthening, and fostering unity. That's the essence of it. When I go outside and ask my son what he did today, I'm not questioning whether he was lazy. I'm trying to build a deeper connection with him and start an open dialogue where he feels my genuine interest in his day.

You cannot build meaningful connections if you're not willing to dive deeper and peel back the layers of the people you're connected to, both personally and professionally. Surface-level interactions lead to service-level relationships. Those who fail to open up and share a part of themselves usually struggle to find the level of success they hope to achieve.

Don't enter a relational field unless you're prepared to engage deeply, as this will only lead to frustration. Even if you're in a job where you answer to no one and are driving solo, it's essential to remain curious. Curiosity could be the very thing standing between you and your next promotion or career opportunity.

Curiosity builds knowledge. For anyone reading this who believes their product will sell itself without any curiosity, I urge you to ask your clients how they feel about it.

Building relationships is crucial. When I moved to Philadelphia with my wife and didn't know anyone, I worked hard to foster those connections. When I met people, they often had no idea I was in staffing initially. We'd go to their homes for cocktails, and eventually, they'd ask what I did. I'd casually mention that I sold IT consulting, often as an afterthought. The focus was on building a genuine relationship.

Recently, I reconnected with a friend from Philadelphia after seven or eight years. It felt like we had just spoken yesterday. She was one of my first clients, and our conversation felt like catching up with an old friend. That's what being curious can bring you—relationships that last.

Whether it's curiosity helping us work through our defensive postures at times or helping us uncover the true needs of a client, curiosity is critical. Curiosity is the key that lets you into a room full of relationships. Use the key, open the door, what you'll find are lasting relationships and a better understanding of this world.

CHAPTER 4

Approachable: What's your Mindset

HOW MANY TIMES HAVE you walked into a room, whether it be a business meeting or a family event, and immediately been able to tell who was more approachable than others within the room? Approachability is an attribute that leads others to you and keeps them engaged. It is an attribute that can be clearly seen on a person's face. Entering rooms with a smile and commanding engagement are clear indicators of approachability. Being viewed as an approachable person opens up a plethora of opportunities, both personally and professionally. Being approachable can kick-start a dynamic conversation. Entering a space without approachable energy will leave you walking away with very little. Conversations will not start, and doors cannot open without an element of approachability.

Having an approachable mindset is something you need to maintain throughout the day, every day. Let me state for the record that that is much easier said than done. Although you may feel you are naturally approachable, it is a discipline you must be aware of when entering social interactions. If you have a bad morning, it may unconsciously affect your mood and therefore your approachability. However, with focus and a bit of practice, you can become much more approachable throughout your day. It can impact every interaction you have.

I want you to think about something while reading this: How long can you carry a smile? When you smile while approaching someone who doesn't have a smile on their face, curiosity comes into play. You don't know why they're not smiling, but it makes them seem unapproachable. This situation can shut down future communication, as they might not look like someone you want to approach and talk to.

However, you also don't know what they're going through. They might be the kindest person on the planet, but they could have what some call a "resting [insert gender] face." This experience happens throughout both your professional and personal life, with everyone you encounter: strangers, people who work in the service industry, your family members, your friends, your colleagues, your coworkers, clients, and your consultants. Therefore, many people that you'll come in contact with will have to be quickly gauged for approachability. There are strategies that help break that down to better understand what's behind the face you're walking up to.

I advise those around me about the importance of approachability. It's essential to remember that when you're engaging with someone, you are aiming to connect with them on a human level. Whether at a gas station, the movies, or the mall, everyone deserves respect, a point I'll elaborate on later.

If you're smiling and they're smiling, you'll find that the interaction will go much more smoothly and can ultimately lead to a meaningful conversation and positive human interaction. It's also crucial for you to read the room and the person you're communicating with. If someone starts off approachable but then seems to withdraw, indicated by their body language, you'll know you've stepped off course.

So, be genuine, and continue being genuine. Constantly read the energy of the person in front of you. Being genuine also means you must listen actively. Approach interactions without an agenda; your goal should simply be to learn, engage, and build camaraderie. That is what being approachable is all about.

Approachable individuals have no hidden agenda. You can often spot people with an agenda from a mile away. As a sophomore in high school, I began to develop a skill I wasn't even aware I was building at the time. I discovered that while hard work was important, it was also essential to connect with my teachers and go out of my way to show them my efforts. I observed that when my teachers recognized my dedication, whether it was through asking questions, staying late, or arriving early, they would guide me toward the right answers. This made me realize that I could achieve good grades not just by performing well on tests, but by demonstrating my hard work in class and having the teachers acknowledge it. I took pride in being recognized as the "biggest teacher's pet," because it meant I worked to engage with them and show my dedication.

It wasn't just about striving for a good grade; I realized that my personality was helping me along the way. It's essential to never fear those who may hold a higher status or title than you. They put on their shoes just like you and me.

Impostor syndrome affects both personal and professional life. You're reading a book by someone who uses impostor syndrome as a strength; I don't see it as a weakness at all, and here's why. When I walk into a room, I aim to learn and earn the respect of those around me. I don't carry a title with me into such situations. It's important to never let someone else's title interfere with your desire to engage with them. This has been true for me in my professional life as well. Regardless of your position in a company, being approachable is essential.

While at the Eight Eleven Group, I enjoyed working with new employees in our organization. They had just graduated from college, often excelling academically, but they may not yet have understood what life would throw at them; it wouldn't always be easy.

Approachability is key. Consider how people can follow leaders who are unapproachable. Leaders who lack approachability rarely succeed in their roles. You must cultivate an approachable demeanor, especially during stressful times, which is something I learned from my experiences in Detroit and Philadelphia, where I built markets from the ground up. If I approached a day with a negative attitude, my unapproachability would overshadow everything. People would focus on why I was upset, and I realized I couldn't allow that to happen.

It's crucial to check those negative feelings at the door. Your approachability should carry a positive tone; otherwise, you risk ruining your next interaction. You can often sense unapproachability from a distance. Remember, approachability is not just a marketing strategy. You need to be warm with clients, approachable to peers and leaders, and friendly toward coworkers. If you're not naturally warm, that's okay. The more you can open up and smile, the more likely it is that you'll foster friendships and professional relationships.

Always maintain a mindset of humility, even if you are at the top of your company. Personally, I've always viewed my title as something that doesn't elevate me above others in this world. While it may bring a sense of pride, particularly to show my late father what I had accomplished, it never influenced how I interacted with people. As you read this book, keep in mind that I am still a person working on myself.

You should strive to maintain a sense of normalcy, even in a high-ranking position. Leaders, let go of your ego; it hinders your approachability. You can often detect an elitist mindset when someone approaches you in a condescending manner. I've encountered people who expect others to stand when they enter a room simply because they hold a title. Sure, their title might be one of prestige, but what message does it send when you demand such a thing? That person has made clear that they have a limited scope of approachability. Again, this can be a byproduct of impostor syndrome creeping in, but it's okay to step into a room with the mindset that you should aim to learn from everyone, regardless of their title.

I've done this my entire life and will continue to do so. I believe it keeps me grounded and fosters my curiosity to learn.

I have really gotten into *Yellowstone*, the TV show, and it was a significant experience for me. One of the statements made in the show really resonated: "You don't deserve it. No one deserves it." This was said to a young character, emphasizing that life's rewards aren't simply given; you have to earn everything. Nothing is handed to you.

When building a business from the ground up, it's crucial to be approachable with everyone you meet. This is why this attribute connects personal and professional aspects of life. It's like a choreographed dance between both lifestyles that I navigate every day.

A personal tool, which I will elaborate on in my next attribute, is the "mirror test." This involves looking at yourself in the mirror before entering a room. When you're speaking to someone, are you aware of how you're presenting yourself? Are you carrying a smile? Even after an initial conversation, maintaining a smile can leave a positive impression. People will remember you as someone who seemed upbeat. That energy is what fosters approachability.

So, remember: don't lead with your wallet; lead with your head and heart. Enter situations with openness and a true desire to connect with others, and you never know how far it can take you. That's the essence of being approachable.

How can you tell when someone enters a situation with an agenda? They tend to walk up to you without really paying attention to what you say. They're usually looking for the leader in the room or the person with the most status. They're trying to connect with the most important individual, focusing on checking off the boxes of their business agenda instead of being genuine. Everyone in the room can spot them, and they are typically the least approachable people in it.

I recently attended an after-hours networking event, so it was more of a social setting. I was introduced to a high-level sales leader who had a pretty aggressive personality. He seemed approachable yet wanted to give off an aura of intensity, and that "closing the deal" was everything. Furthermore, when in front of clients, he only wanted to know the "no" in the room, the undecided decision-makers.

That was it.

His agenda was narrow in scope, and I was thinking the entire time about how the rest of those clients felt in the room when he was using this approach. His agenda was very intent on closing the deal. During this conversation, nothing was discussed about the client, their needs, or whether they really needed the product in the first place.

I share this story because my approach is to win the deal, but not at the cost of burning a lasting relationship or forcing a product on a client knowing it's not needed or that it's incompatible with a client's ecosystem. It's sometimes hard to watch. They are not reading the room. They are not there to genuinely engage and learn.

I hope that everyone in the sales industry (leaders included) understands that avoiding a rigid agenda is crucial. Throughout my twenty-five years in this industry, I rarely approached any meeting with a predetermined agenda. You never know what someone might be going through before they walk into a meeting or what could be on their mind.

Don't get me wrong, I had an outline, and I absolutely wanted to learn about the client and their environment, but it was a blank page because I didn't know where the meeting would go. I wanted to try to achieve some of those notes that I had marked down in my meeting prep. At the end of these meetings, I would also ask for feedback, which was the final feedback loop of approachability in that meeting. How they felt about the interaction was immediate feedback I got by simply asking. That's why approachability is vital to lasting human connection and tied to all professional success stories.

It's essential to be approachable. You don't know what might have happened before they arrived, which could explain the frown on their face. When you're running a business and trying to inspire others to follow your lead, it's vital to maintain an approachable demeanor. If you're not approachable, you'll struggle to get anyone to join you and work toward a common goal.

So, can you have an agenda yet still be approachable? Of course, you can, but you have to understand that the agenda and how that meeting might go, or how your day might go, could change. Things happen, as life normally does. If you're solely working off an agenda and a curveball gets thrown, how do you handle it? That's why if you stay approachable and carry a loose agenda, so to speak, you're ready for the curveball if it's thrown your way.

Agendas that assist with approachability can be very helpful, especially in tackling difficult conversations. It's helpful to let the other person know upfront that the discussion might be a bit tougher than usual. This way, they understand the context and can prepare themselves mentally. Essentially, it's about setting the right tone for the conversation.

I had an agenda to grow every market I entered, but when I was in front of a client, they never perceived my agenda as simply trying to secure a business deal right then and there. Instead, my true agenda was to learn and understand. I aimed to be genuine, shared my story, and built a friendship.

Yes, having an agenda is acceptable. Great people who are truly focused on establishing meaningful relationships don't overtly show it. Ultimately, when you break it down, my goal was to form a connection with you. Maybe you'll buy something, and maybe you won't, but I find you interesting, and I genuinely want to build a relationship.

I can relate to this sentiment from personal and professional experience. At the first major sales conference I attended with my previous company, everyone around me advised against introducing myself to the CEO, the owner, or the founder of the company. I won't name names, but it was a massive billion-dollar company, and they were all arriving around 10:30 or 11:00 p.m. In the lobby, everyone told me, "Don't go up and say anything. Please don't introduce yourself."

I thought to myself, *Why wouldn't I take this opportunity?* So, I made the decision to walk right up to him. He was smoking a cigar and had a commanding presence. I approached him and said, "Hey, I'm Jonathan Eldridge. Nice to meet you. I'm from the Grand Rapids market."

To my surprise, he was very friendly and responded, "Nice to meet you, Jonathan. How are you?"

I had an agenda to show no fear, use approachability, and perhaps be remembered. While I accomplished the first two, I'm not sure he remembered me. I definitely remembered, and I guess that's what matters.

Meanwhile, I could see the others watching, likely wishing they had seized that moment instead of holding back. To me, it didn't matter how important he was; I wasn't going to let that stop me from introducing myself. Afterward, some people who had initially thought I was making a mistake came up to me, asking, "Did you really shake his hand? You did? That's awesome!" I could tell they regretted not stepping up themselves.

In the end, I felt proud that I took the chance. It was a great experience, and I encouraged them to be more open to moments like that in the future.

So what do you do when you hear someone say they *deserve* _____?

When people tell me that they deserve something, I often ask them why they feel that way. I want to understand what makes them think they deserve it.

To deserve something is to say that you're almost entitled to it, worthy of it. In contrast, *earned* implies effort and straight-up "elbow grease"; some might call it "grit." Those efforts earn the reward. Much like my *Yellowstone* quote, if you go about your day with a sense of having to earn it, respecting the time you have, and the relationships you're cultivating, being approachable is a must.

They might say something like, "Well, you know, I've worked hard." And I respond, "Okay, but everyone has worked hard. Give me more than that. Did you put in extra work? Did you come in early and stay late? Did you show initiative? Did you work on weekends? Did you go above and beyond what was asked of you? Did you truly earn that position through your efforts?"

There are many people in the sales industry who walk into a thriving territory and easily get business, thinking, *Wow, this is so easy—sales is a piece of cake.* But then there are those who start in a brand-new territory where no one knows them. They have to hustle, face challenges, and earn their place, often getting bruised and battered in the process. Those are the people I want on my team every day of the week and twice on Sunday, because they know what it means to truly earn their success.

So, to anyone stepping into a vibrant territory, I would say: you need to figure out how to earn your place, because you were handed an advantage that others had to work hard to achieve. The approachability of clients in a vibrant territory is very different from the approachability of clients in an untouched territory. So you'd better bring that smile on your face.

To summarize approachability: it's not only about the energy you carry when you walk into a room. It's also about being able to measure the approachability of those around you. Familiar clients may feel more approachable because they are already familiar with your sales process and your services. New clients may feel less approachable because the relationship is new, and they are more skeptical. Your approachability when you enter these situations can steer the direction of the relationship. Understand your client, but be flexible. Enter into your client interactions with a smile and an eagerness to understand them better, and you will find that you will be remembered for all the right reasons.

CHAPTER 5

Authenticity: The Currency of Today

AUTHENTICITY IS TRULY what sets you apart. It represents energy at full thrust. When you believe in what you say, others believe in what they hear. Authentic individuals reveal their worth through their everyday actions.

This concept is where true greatness emerges. It's not about endlessly pursuing greatness; instead, it's about being genuinely authentic. Authenticity is my premier attribute within this framework, among the twelve I discuss. It's the innate attribute that you don't need to try to work at. It's your superpower, and not only creates lasting impressions, but makes sure they're retained too.

What do authentic people bring to the table? Being authentic is today's currency. It can be the deciding factor between being recognized and remembered or being just another person who drops a voicemail or sits in a client's office participating in a standard, forgettable meeting, versus someone who leaves a lasting impression.

Impostor syndrome can complicate this attribute. I've experienced it throughout my life; I often walk into a room feeling inadequate and wanting/needing to earn my place. And there's nothing wrong with that. It will keep you level, balanced, and most importantly, yourself.

Authentic people possess an innate belief in their relational abilities to connect with others. I have always felt this way, able to get along with my teachers, coaches, bosses, and mentors. I learned from these individuals, all of whom embodied authenticity themselves. My coach during elementary and high school was exceptionally genuine; he understood when he was instructing as a teacher, coaching as an athletic mentor, or simply being a friend. This was crucial for my development.

Understanding my *why* and recognizing that my personal story could enhance my career became imperative. I often told my managers and colleagues that I didn't go to Central Michigan University to learn how to take advantage of people. That mindset simply isn't part of my character.

I also realized that authentic people are comfortable being vulnerable, and that vulnerability is perfectly acceptable, as long as it's balanced. It's important to read the room. There are managers who may not appreciate vulnerability, while others embrace it. Authentic individuals can gauge the atmosphere, noticing the mannerisms and curiosity levels of those they interact with, and share their vulnerabilities accordingly.

I've stood on stages in front of hundreds of people, openly sharing my weaknesses. This vulnerability makes me more relatable, and relatability is a major facet of authenticity.

Being around others energizes me. It takes me back to childhood. That energy is intrinsic to who I am. Many have remarked, "I'm not sure if it's authentic or what, but this guy has a lot of energy," and this has always been true for me. It remains true today and will continue until my final day. Much of this energy stems from the pain I've endured; I channel that pain and use it as fuel, allowing me to feel liberated and function effectively.

Laughing, smiling, and engaging with others makes people comfortable so that they too can be themselves. When someone is open with me, it inspires me to be more open too, leading to great conversations and relationships rooted in sincerity and heart.

When I say that people energize me and help me feel free, I'm expressing who I am at my core. Some might interpret my enthusiasm as cheesy, but most would say I genuinely love making people laugh and smile. That's why giving keynote speeches and writing this book are so important to me. The stories that we share, of our successes as well as our failures, connect us humans. Being able to laugh and smile through all of those moments and see a little bit of ourselves in each other is an authentic experience.

Life isn't just about winning the day; it's about living it. My life's struggles have shaped me and made me stronger, allowing me to share my experiences. Sharing has increased my authenticity, and as I've grown older, I've become even more open about my journey. I love mentoring and coaching because my story can help others navigate their own challenges.

Authenticity is a vital trait of professional leaders; they naturally light up a room. I realized that being authentic meant I wasn't just promoting my company, I was promoting myself and my purpose. Why am I here? Why do I strive to build a business or support a community? It's because I live life with the goal of helping others foster deeper connections based on the core pillars of communication.

Understanding that life is finite motivates me to consider what legacy I will leave behind. I openly share my *why*. I share my experiences with divorce, getting remarried, losing my brother, growing up with little means while surrounded by wealth, because these are my authentic life experiences. They have shaped the man I am and the professional I continue to strive to be. These experiences help me identify with others both personally and professionally.

Ultimately, you are always selling yourself. If people don't see you as genuine, they won't buy from you. Authenticity comes from believing in what you sell and standing behind it. I am committed to following through for others, knowing I won't be perfect. If you're looking for perfection, you are on a fool's quest. Authentic people are not perfect and often share their imperfections.

In your job, your first priority should be to learn first, sell second. This aligns with Dale Carnegie's principles: learn first, act second, and start with the end in mind. Authentic individuals are genuinely curious and eager to learn more about others.

To test your authenticity, try this exercise: after finishing this chapter, put the book down, go to your bathroom, turn off the light, and give your best pitch about who you are or why you want to meet that manager, completely in the dark. Then, turn the light on while doing it in front of yourself. Now you're staring at the person who might purchase from you down the road, someone who is judging your every mannerism.

Are you smiling? Are you using the proper inflection? Do you actually look authentically approachable, as we just discussed?

Light on, light off. In life, you don't get the chance to have the lights off unless you're practicing because, in reality, the light is always on. You need to be able to hit that note consistently and be aware of what you look like while doing it.

Authentic people practice that. I am still practicing the mirror test today. Before I give a keynote or have an important interaction, I often go into the bathroom to look at myself and ensure I'm showing positivity.

Try it. It works, and you will be surprised by how much you can learn about yourself during this exercise.

Then burn your scripted material. Life is not scripted. A long time ago, when I was a regional manager at Brooksource (the largest of the family of companies within Eight Eleven). I went into the Columbus market and found myself sitting across from a new recruiter. The office was full, and there weren't many available seats, so I had to sit directly across from him for the entire day. He was extremely nervous to sit across from me because of my title.

This guy had been leaving great messages all day long, but when I got up to see what he was doing, I discovered he had been reading from a script the whole time. I thought, *My God, he didn't switch it up at all.*

So, in the middle of his next voicemail, I literally grabbed his script and ripped it up. He stumbled through his message but eventually got through it. When he hung up the phone, he asked, "What are you doing?" I replied, "Hey, listen, you can't use a script. Life isn't going to provide you with a script to follow. What if the manager doesn't like what you're saying, and that script was wrong all day? You've just been repeating it."

Whenever I went to different markets, I would encourage all the employees to go home and leave a voicemail for themselves. This isn't the Progressive commercial, I promise. The next day, we'd come in and play them on speaker to evaluate how they sounded.

When we did that, this young recruit's message was the last one played, and it outshined all the others, even from very tenured, professional, and accomplished salespeople. He had a tear in his eye, and I almost shed a tear for him because he finally got it. He realized it wasn't about the script; it was about being unscripted.

It was about understanding that you don't need to read off material. No, you need to be yourself. Authentic people sell themselves, and everything else will follow.

The main idea is that if you engage with all aspects of a conversation effectively, you can reach a flow state. This allows you to connect in a way that makes you memorable to others. That's the key point.

If you're going to sit at a bar and talk about the positive attributes at five o'clock on a Friday, life must be good. Honestly, think about it: when was the last time you witnessed two people arguing about things like approachability and relatability?

That kind of conversation doesn't happen often, but if it did, our world would be in a much better place. Personally, I get energized by these discussions. You could say I get a bit wound up because, yes, I didn't graduate with a 4.0 GPA. But I'll be damned if I'm not going to be the hardest-working, most energized person in every room I enter. I strive to be that way because of the losses I've experienced and what I've been through. It's not about winning; it's about working to be the best version of yourself and sharing that person with the world.

If you find yourself struggling to make those genuine connections, try becoming more authentic, and you will find that doors of opportunity will open. Look for a handshake and a hug, not just a contract.

There are many people in my past company with whom I will be friends for life, even if we don't talk often. One of my past coworkers (vice president of Calculated Hire), Robert "Bobby" Bauscher, is one of those people. If you ask anyone in the company, they will tell you that Bobby is genuine and authentic. I would describe Bobby as one of the most authentic people I know, because he has the ability to light up a room. When I hear stories about past events, my first question is often, "Was Bobby there?" He is the type of person you are better for being around. He has incredible energy, and people are drawn to it. The root of that energy is authenticity.

Bobby and I have talked about this a lot, and funnily enough, he is even better at it than I am. This sometimes frustrates me, because he truly is one of the most authentically wonderful people you'll ever meet. He can make you laugh and even bring you to tears with his sincerity. He is hardworking, driven, and charismatic.

There's a reason why he is the VP of Calculated Hire. He understands who he is and is willing to share that with those around him. He has been able to excel professionally and create a tremendous family while staying true to himself.

I want to emphasize the importance of staying true to yourself and remaining authentic. More than a decade ago, seven of us were in an executive meeting, trying to figure out how to run the company. This was before I quit drinking. I used to be sometimes overly boisterous and loud, sometimes even obnoxious. But I always got my point across because I was passionate about what I was discussing.

During that meeting, we were giving each other advice on how to improve, and one of my peers had some feedback for me. I was curious about what he would say. He said, "Jonathan, honestly, you're the Howard Stern of staffing." Everyone burst into laughter because it's true, I don't have a filter. I can't always be perfect or professional.

But my other coworkers considered my approach, although sometimes unconventional, to be authentic. I took it as a compliment, but he also cautioned me that while it's good to be authentic, you don't want to ruin your brand by going too far or saying too much. Staying balanced and measured throughout conversations is key. Keep your energy in line with the conversation you are having.

So, how do you keep yourself from going too far or saying too much? That's where the prep comes in. Understanding *the person* you're meeting with. You can gauge a lot from simply reviewing a LinkedIn profile. This provides insights, like their years of experience, which industries they have been a part of professionally, their personal backgrounds, and interests. There is a treasure trove of information at your fingertips if you take the initiative and do your homework. Be diligent to try to understand as much as you can about *the person* you're meeting with, not just the client.

If you prepare for challenges and alternate scenarios before they arise, you'll be better equipped to handle them if things don't go as planned. Being proactive allows you to tackle issues more effectively and not just respond impulsively. So, make sure to do the necessary work in advance.

I often explain to a manager what they can expect from me. I outline what they'll see and who I am. I think this is important in both professional and personal interactions. You don't need to pretend; lay the groundwork for the communication style your managers are going to be interacting with.

Not everyone is comfortable being transparent about who they are when meeting someone new. There are people who may seem intimidating, but once you approach them with a question, you'll find that they can be very conversational. It all relates back to being approachable. When you combine these elements, you can grow and improve as a person and in your profession.

As you read through this book and its chapters, realize that if you embody the attributes discussed, you can achieve and accomplish more than you ever thought possible.

Looking back, I can say that I definitely didn't do everything perfectly. I always aspired to be my best, but being flawed is a part of being authentic. Being open and honest about my flaws and failures has allowed people around me to feel more comfortable in my presence. When you use this approach both personally and professionally, you will find that it is easier to build organic relationships because no one has to pretend.

Humor is essential. The more you can laugh at yourself and approach situations with humor, the more authentic you become. Human connection is formed through the acknowledgment that there are common threads that weave us all together. We have all tried and failed. We have all had days so bad you had to laugh in order not to cry. Finding those connections is what draws people together and ultimately begins the relationship-building process.

I am not just about selling brochures; I am a relationship builder and have found success because of it. There are many "leaders and salespeople" out there, but the ones who focus only on their agenda and the profit don't foster authenticity.

Authentic people prepare themselves emotionally and mentally. They can read the room and understand the limits. Being able to read situations is an innate skill in authentic relationship-building. Learning how to gauge a situation and understanding when to push farther or when to fall back is a key element. This ability will help you connect with others, even when interacting through a screen.

Start sharing *you* with your clients. Believe in what you're trying to achieve/sell. Tell your story, share your *why*. Be genuine and communicate your intention. Authenticity is remembered, and that's where true human connection begins. You can use it to grow stronger relationships throughout your life, both personally and professionally.

CHAPTER 6

Adaptable: Tackling the Day-to-Day

IN THE PAST TWO AND A HALF YEARS, I have undergone four total knee replacements. You don't need me to do the math to understand that that's a few too many. I had replacements on both knees, but unfortunately, there were complications that led to both of them needing to be "revised." Revised is the surgical term for "the replacement for the replacement."

As a highly active fifty-year-old man with two teenage boys, this was devastating news. I have had to learn how to walk again four different times. I've been under anesthesia for a total of eighteen hours over the past two and a half years. This, obviously, took a tremendous toll on me physically, emotionally, and mentally. I struggled with the adjustment of having to rely so heavily on others to help me. After spending my life caring for others, facing my own health challenges turned my world upside down. I thought I would recover after the first surgery and continue with my normal life, but my journey took me down a very different path. Believe me, one major surgery was enough, but four in such a short timespan was absolutely life-altering.

This experience was tough not only for me but also for my kids, my wife, my career, and my relationships with others. Knee replacements are pretty common nowadays. Everyone around you tells you it will be fine, and you will be feeling great in no time. But what if that isn't the case? I definitely did not have your "typical" experience, and I was definitely not fine. Of course, people are kind and they try to offer words of encouragement, but they couldn't truly understand the magnitude of what I was facing. Of course, they did not understand what it was like to feel trapped in a body that didn't feel like my own. Of course, they did not know how difficult it was to learn to walk again, four times over. Could anyone do this and truly stay positive?

In addition to my knee surgeries, there was also a period between my third and fourth operations where I was diagnosed with skin cancer. This resulted in an additional procedure above my lip in which all of the cancerous tissue was removed. This was, obviously, a shocking diagnosis to receive in addition to my other medical challenges. I wasn't prepared for the mental toll or the physical scar this would leave.

Adaptability has been essential in all these experiences. I had to learn to stop mourning what I couldn't do and embrace what I could. This hadn't been the plan, but it was the road I had to walk. I could have easily fallen into a "poor me" or "why did this happen to me?" mindset, but I leaned into the mindset of being adaptable. There are so many elements in life that are simply beyond our control, but how we choose to tackle them is our choice. You can stay stuck, or you can adapt.

Another significant life change I made was to quit drinking. I thought drinking made me the life of the party. I thought it added to my persona of being energetic and fun. It took me many years to realize that my relationship with alcohol was unhealthy and that it ultimately did not serve me. I realized I didn't need alcohol to enjoy life.

I now face the challenge of building relationships based on genuine friendship, rather than on shared drinking experiences. Most of my previous relationships revolved around outings that included drinking. Learning to navigate my social life without alcohol has been a massive adaptation, and it's one that many people still struggle to understand. It has been interesting to see how many people around me have struggled to adapt and accept my choice. I am still the same person. I am still loud, energetic, and fun. It has been an eye-opening transition, and it isn't always easy to navigate, but I am proud of the progress I've made.

Being adaptable is a daily necessity. You can create a to-do list, but it's important to recognize that things may not go as planned. In moments of stress, fear, or anxiety, that's when everyone looks to the calm leader, someone who knows how to adapt. I strive to show my sons that adaptability is crucial every day.

A few months ago, I went for a walk with my wife, and I brought along a list of my CARE card attributes. I had her guess my scores on a twelve-point scale, one point for each attribute. I thought I was at eleven or twelve, but she pointed out that I needed to work on my adaptability at home. She said that while I may project calmness and adaptability at work, I often struggle with it at home. I hadn't realized that before, but it highlighted how this framework can be applied both personally and professionally.

I didn't create this *Soul Focus* CARE Framework solely for professional success. The program also has significant implications for personal growth and longevity. It's essential to understand that in life, even when you have everything planned out, things might not unfold as you envisioned. Since that walk with my wife, I have been more mindful of being adaptable in all areas of my life.

I made adaptability a key focus of my personal improvement plan within my framework. It's an area where I needed to grow, and I've seen progress because I had my partner point out where I could improve. It was fantastic to involve my two teenagers in the framework as well. They are now grading and testing each other on how they can improve. It's impressive to see them working on these attributes at such a young age. When I was fifteen, no one was helping me learn how to be more approachable or how important it was to connect with people around me on a deeper level. The fact that my boys are realizing that respect is unconditional and that we must be adaptable and consistent is significant. They're discussing these attributes, which are helping them become better young men.

My point in sharing my journey, including my knee replacements and challenges mentioned at the start of this chapter, is that I had to adapt. Everyone reading this book has likely faced struggles, whether it's dealing with a loss, medical challenges, or other personal issues. Those who manage to come through often find newfound joy and a passion for making the most out of life. That is the power of learning to adapt.

Someone once told me that my knee replacements were just a moment in time. However, they turned out to be two and a half years of intense pain and worries about infections and complications. It wasn't easy, but I had to adapt. I had to adjust to being cared for, relying on my kids to bring me dinner or take the dog out, and handling tasks I couldn't do at that time. As I made progress, I had to continually adapt to my limitations and embrace my progress one step at a time.

In any profession, especially in consulting, we face highs and lows daily. How do you handle these challenges? Do you go for a walk? Do you talk things through with someone? Educating yourself and preparing for potential challenges is the best way to cultivate adaptability.

At the age of twenty-six, I went through a tremendous amount of change in both my personal and professional life. It was time for a rebuild. That was my moment of starting over and reconnecting with Ryan Hasbrook, co-founder of the Eight Eleven Group.

I was at my lowest point financially. Taking bottles back for cash at the age of twenty-six felt like rock bottom. I was in the midst of adapting to a different future for myself. I was creating a fresh start both in my personal and professional life. Starting over in my profession meant taking a risk and building a new business from scratch in Detroit. Even while going through personal challenges, I realized I could make this work. There was nothing stopping me. My mindset and relational skills could drive my success.

This was my chance to rebuild my life. Through dedication and hard work, the Detroit market took off. None of that would have been possible if I had not been able to adapt. There were mountains of challenges between me and success, but I was able to tackle each one because I was always able to adjust and make the necessary pivots needed to overcome them.

Just when I felt like I had reached a comfortable level of success in Detroit, I received a call from Ryan asking me to head to Philadelphia to stabilize and grow our East Coast operations. It felt like a monumental task. Starting one company from scratch was tough enough, and now I was being asked to do it again in a different city.

Philadelphia had briefly opened with a couple of employees, but it really needed to be established from the ground up. After much consideration, my wife and I decided to make the move to the East Coast. It was a huge decision, probably the most important one in my career. I was leaving behind everything I had ever known to create my own lasting legacy within the organization.

The East Coast is a beast, and it came with its own set of unique challenges. I had to learn the culture of the business there quickly and adapt to the pace and demands of that region. I remember my first time at a Wawa gas station, asking where the "pop" was, only to nearly get kicked out of the Wawa for using the term. You can't say "pop" on the East Coast: it's soda out there! It was a very literal "We aren't in Kansas anymore" moment.

Adapting is crucial in sales. The mindset of selling to a manager in the Midwest is entirely different from selling to a manager on the East Coast. In the Midwest, they appreciate a relational approach and value time spent getting to know them. On the East Coast, however, time is of the essence. They want results quickly; it's all about return on time (ROT).

It's vital to understand that you have to be willing to adapt to succeed. This industry can chew you up and spit you out if you're resistant to change. Leaders and salespeople must modify their style and never stick to a single script. I realized that each "no" I encountered was an opportunity to deepen my curiosity and explore other areas of the business.

Transitioning from the number one technical staffing company in the nation to building something new with Ryan and Jeff out of Indianapolis was a significant adaptation. I went from being recognized by everyone to being relatively unknown, all while facing skeptics who claimed we wouldn't succeed. Regardless, we focused on making it happen.

Reading the room and personally adapting when necessary is incredibly important. In fact, adaptability is the second corporate attribute within the corporate CARE equation. Every company needs to adapt, whether in pharmaceuticals, healthcare, product manufacturing, or service delivery. If companies cannot respond to market volatility, they become stagnant, like being stuck in quicksand.

Clients' needs can change abruptly. Sometimes those changes can occur halfway through a proposal—or worse, when the invoice is due and they want to renegotiate terms. Organizations that can adapt and lead within their industries typically become trendsetters. The first essential attribute is consistency, and the second is adaptability.

To be successful in any industry, you must be adaptable. There have been many situations in my career where I've had to change and adjust my approach. Those who are rigid and refuse to adjust their approach or mindset will find themselves losing out on key opportunities. To me, if you're not adapting, then you are stagnant. You are robbing yourself of the opportunity to grow. Adapting will always be essential when navigating the challenges life gives us.

I had a coworker take my CARE card home and give it to her husband, who was applying for medical school. He wanted to improve his communication skills and used my twelve-attribute CARE Framework to better understand how to interview. She went through it with him, providing an outline that highlighted important attributes to work on in preparation for his medical school interviews.

As a result of focusing on these twelve attributes, he improved his interviewing skills and successfully gained admission to medical school. He was able to successfully work the CARE program and adapt his interview approach. He felt the program process allowed him to easily identify areas for personal improvement and was crucial in helping him make the necessary adjustments for a successful interview. This shows that this framework doesn't just apply to leaders or those in the sales industry. Anyone looking to better identify their own areas of core strengths and weaknesses in the pursuit of self-improvement will benefit from this program.

People have asked if these attributes are more important at home or at work: "Can I get away with applying this discipline in one area of my life?" The question you should really be asking yourself is, *Why would I want to?* These attributes are equally important both in the workplace and in your personal life, and can only benefit you when applied universally. When exercising these skills regularly, you will find them to feel like second nature.

Personal growth is essential for professional development. I have yet to see someone advance professionally without first growing personally. If you can show me a professional who hasn't improved personally, I'll show you a buffalo nickel (and that's something I've never seen before). It doesn't happen the other way around. Historically, you will find that companies that pour into their people and have an invested interest in their personal growth will yield much more success.

When starting this new venture, I was very focused on a company name that would personify my vision for what this program could offer to the world. I landed on "Soul Focus" because your focus on life and the pursuit of growth and relationships starts from within, from the *soul*.

Personal Development = Professional Success.

If your day, your week, or your month has started off rough and you're trying to regain consistency, adapt and consider setting both personal and professional goals. In these moments, it's time to recalibrate yourself. By doing this, you're likely to become more consistent and feel a greater sense of accomplishment throughout the day. Being adaptable is key.

Talk about being able to adapt, I would come home from my days in Detroit, and Danielle could see the exhaustion on my face. She could tell that the pressure of building a market and what this entailed was taking its toll. I obviously wanted the market to succeed and to help those around me achieve their own professional goals.

She would remind me, "Dude, Rome wasn't built in a day." Relationships take time. Plant your seeds, and the garden will grow. Sometimes in our race to succeed, we can forget that the road can be long. The mountains will be high. Building a business is hard. Having four knee replacements was really hard. Whatever hard thing you are working to overcome may not be done quickly. That is okay. Take the challenges that come and adapt. *Adapting* gives you the power to put one foot in front of the other and continue to move forward.

For years, I'd wake up and write a list of things to do. I had to physically write it down, even though I already knew what I needed to accomplish. It was the act of writing it down that made it feel like a real call to action. Funny enough, I would often finish that list by noon. So I adapted and set goals that could expand throughout the day!

You have to set goals that can be accomplished in a 24-hour period. Managing expectations is crucial. If you have to adjust your goals accordingly, adjust them and adapt so that you can still have a sense of accomplishing the goals for the day. You have to adapt and set realistic expectations.

My "live the day" approach fuels me with energy and gives me the power to adapt. Life is precious and fleeting. If you take anything from this, hug your wife, hug your kids, hug your mom and dad, and your siblings. Be genuine in every interaction you have, and be ready to adapt to whatever comes your way. It starts with adapting at home, setting realistic goals that can be modified based on your interactions and what you're trying to achieve that day. Adaptability can read the room and help be the thermostat that levels out a challenging situation. This skill is vital to growing successful businesses and lasting relationships.

CHAPTER 7

Respect: It's Unconditional and Should Go Without Saying

RESPECT IS AN UNCONDITIONAL piece of any successful relationship, both personally and professionally. As I was developing this CARE Framework and establishing my R's, the word "respect" came to me immediately. You might think it's an obvious choice, but I have seen respect overlooked or not given. Sometimes respect can be fake, and the false illusion can be used to manipulate or appease those around us. Respect is a product of integrity and trust. Respect can be seen, heard, and felt. Respect is not always a two-way street. Sometimes it is given and not received. Respect is always the goal and the solid foundation on which a comprehensive relationship is built.

Disrespect can damage relationships and lead to misinformation and judgment. There are countless disrespectful acts that can occur in a day, which is why respect must be an attribute we continuously stay focused on and work to develop.

As you may have gathered, I am the "middle child" in my family. Coming from a household with limited resources and having friends with varying socioeconomic backgrounds, I learned that everyone was looking through different lenses. We may have been going through the same things, but not necessarily having the exact same experience.. As a child, I couldn't control where I came from or how much money my family had. I could control things like how I presented myself and my work ethic, which led to me earning respect from friends and family. This shaped my view on respect. I never felt anyone was "better" than anyone else, regardless of where they came from. Every single person deserved respect.

What defines respect in a relationship? Are the people in your life respectful? Do they respond to you in a timely manner? Do they value your time? Did they prepare for the meeting they have with you today?

There are ways to measure respect both personally and professionally, and it is essential to recognize that respect must be unconditional. I must show respect to my children and my wife; in return, I expect (and get) the same. Even though my children learn from me, it's important for me to respect them as well, ensuring that we maintain open lines of communication.

At an early age, I realized how important it was to respect everyone in any situation, at any time. My dad worked as a grocery store manager, and on Friday nights, I could not wait to go in and help him. I would help stock shelves and do pretty much anything he asked me to do. I was always asking questions and learning the business along the way. This grocery store was in a bad part of town, in an area that was quite challenging.

At a very early age, I learned how important it was to engage with everyone regardless of how they looked. Everyone has a story to tell. I learned to engage with people who were different from me, and rather than avoiding them, I made an effort to understand their circumstances.

I have vivid memories from my childhood that emphasize the importance of respect. During holidays, there was often a stranger at our table. Despite our limited means, my mom would seek out individuals in the community who might not have anyone to turn to during the holidays. I remember my mom, God bless her, inviting a stranger over to ensure they had a meal. That act of kindness was a truly respectful act.

Sometimes it can be the smallest of gestures that not only helps a person but also teaches a young eight-year-old boy how important it is to respect everyone. I will never forget one particular day when my mom stopped on the side of the road to help a woman struggling with her groceries. We were a couple of miles from our home, and I was bewildered as she explained her intention to assist the lady. We loaded her groceries into our trunk and drove her home. That moment is a core memory for me; I don't know if my mom recalls it, but I remember how much respect she showed that woman. Later that year, the same woman returned to join us for Thanksgiving dinner.

It really helped ground me in my desire to understand people and recognize that everyone has a story to tell. We all face hardships. Those with even the most severe hardships didn't just end up where they are without a background and a journey that shaped their circumstances.

Society needs to be more respectful and curious about the reasons why people end up in difficult circumstances. Everyone deserves that respect. This is where I found the true impact that my company, Soul Focus, can have during interactions. It's about working with both head and heart. When you engage with someone using both intellect and compassion, it truly makes a difference. This is why I named my company Soul Focus, LLC.

Utilizing both head and heart is essential in every interaction we have throughout the day. By doing so, we consistently show and give respect. Respect can be communicated in various forms. It can be visual, like not having proper eye contact, not sitting up in your chair, or not standing in a lobby before a meeting. Those would be *visual cues* of a lack of respect.

Vocal cues include sighing at the wrong time or being monotone when the conversation has energy and life to it. I'll discuss that later in the book with enthusiasm and eagerness. Those would be vocal cues of a lack of respect.

Finally, there would be **behavioral cues.** A yawn is awful and pretty easily spotted as a lack of respect, because you're not in the moment. In those situations, I suggest you bite your lip, bite your tongue, do whatever you have to do to stop your mouth from yawning. It's happened to everyone. It's happened to me countless times. It's almost as if the manager can see you fighting it back, which would actually show a lack of respect by trying to hold it in, as well as crossing your arms or being a constant interrupter during a conversation. With any one of these actions, you could be sending the wrong message. Those who give respect often demonstrate proactive thought in both their personal actions and professional tasks.

As I mentioned earlier, people who invest thought into their actions respect the processes they are involved in. For example, I respect the daily responsibility of being a father, providing for my family, and fulfilling my obligations at work and home. I recognize that these tasks need to be completed; they are not merely checkboxes to tick off.

Sometimes, it's easier to extend respect when you've personally felt disrespected. I've experienced moments where I felt disrespected or questioned, which caught me off guard since I strive to lead with respect in all my interactions. While it's not always achievable, curiosity can help you uphold respect as a fundamental attribute. Ultimately, respect should be unconditional. It's something everyone deserves unless given a reason not to respect them, much like trust.

This perspective has shaped my leadership style. Respect manifests in various ways: it's seen, heard, and felt. It's about showing up on time, being present in conversations, and going the extra mile for the greater good, without any hidden agenda.

Be kind to everyone you engage with. When I started my journey in Detroit, I would go door-to-door, walking into offices and speaking with receptionists, trying to identify someone in their IT department who might talk to me. Once, I managed to get onto an elevator I wasn't supposed to be on and made my way up to the fourth floor in Dearborn, Michigan, to meet with an automotive marketing company.

I ended up speaking with a receptionist for about half an hour, discussing life and my pursuit of building my company. After our conversation, I returned to my office. Later, I received a phone call from the director of operations. He mentioned that the receptionist had given him my business card and said, "Our receptionist said you were pretty passionate and came across as a genuinely nice guy. I don't have much time, but I have seven needs right now. Can you fill seven QA tester positions?" And while that wasn't our first client in Detroit, that call opened up the door, and we were off to the races. The opportunity was created because I respected the receptionist and took time to get to know her. She then wanted to learn about me and gave me the opportunity to tell my story. Respect brought us our first large client.

I had an eye-opening experience that day that taught me the importance of respect in the workplace. During a conversation with a receptionist who was well-connected within her company, I learned that the reason a director of operations called me was twofold: my competition was complacent, and she thought I was a good person because I treated her kindly. This simple act of respect led to significant opportunities for my business. Within two weeks, we filled seven positions, and over the course of the next two years, we became one of their largest suppliers in Detroit.

Respect is crucial for everyone in an organization, regardless of their role: from the person who cleans the windows to the one who signs your paycheck, to those in the legal department. Everyone deserves respect. Because I showed respect to that receptionist, she handed my card to the right person, which allowed us to make a lasting impact in the Detroit market.

Remember, respect must be shown and earned; it is not simply deserved. How you treat someone today can determine whether they reach out for your services tomorrow. I often remind the people I work with that a consultant today could be a client tomorrow, especially if you treat them well.

You never know who someone is or who they might know. A person you might disregard could be instrumental in your success down the line.

Personally and professionally, I strive to connect with everyone I meet, as you never know where your paths might interconnect in the future.

In my early career, I always emphasized respect for those I worked with. I never wanted anyone working "for" me—they worked "with" me. This mindset applies to every leader. Using "I" in team settings can sound self-centered. It's essential to take ownership as a collective by saying "we failed" instead of pointing fingers and assigning individual blame.

In those early days, I hand-delivered paychecks every Friday. This simple act allowed me to connect with my consultants, thank them for their hard work, and see how they spent their weekends. One day, a manager asked, "Why do you come down here every Friday when you could just use direct deposit?" I replied that I wanted to see my team and express my gratitude, which ultimately led to increased opportunities with one of our first large hospital clients in Philadelphia. I should proudly mention that in the early days at the Eight Eleven Group (before it became too large to encompass geographically), every market hand-delivered paychecks/paystubs for this very reason.

I wanted to emphasize the importance of expressing gratitude, especially toward consultants. A simple "thank you" can have a profound impact on your career and relationships within the workplace. On another day delivering checks, a manager called me into his office and said, "You know, I work with another client who never stops by to see their people. We pay them a significant amount every year, and I feel like I should be giving that money to you if you can provide this level of service." I'll say it again, a simple "thank you" can have a profound impact on your career and relationships within the workplace.

Because I consistently showed respect to my consultants by hand-delivering their pay stubs and thanking them, other managers began noticing this approach and wanted to collaborate with me. This situation reminds me of the "Jerry Maguire effect," where people are drawn to someone who demonstrates a conscience, knows right from wrong, and genuinely wants to do right by others.

The simple act of thanking my consultants helped me build my career and grow the business. I received feedback that I consistently expressed gratitude and was always there to say thank you.

Additionally, remember what I mentioned about waiting in the lobby? Respectful individuals stand eager and anticipatory for the human interaction to come. This kind of respect should be unconditional. It not only wins you business but, more importantly, cultivates meaningful relationships.

So why is it that we sometimes slip up and miss on respect? First off, no one's perfect. Second, we get caught up in our own lives, so focused on our own tasks that we forget to look around at what might be happening around us. This is a very true story that occurred just recently.

On a very hot Saturday afternoon, an older gentleman fell right behind me while watching a baseball game. He collapsed due to a drop in his blood sugar, and I managed to catch him as he fell against the backstop. Immediately, I thought of my dad and sprang into action; this man clearly needed help. He needed to get out of the sun, and I assured him, "I've got you. You won't fall. I will carry you." We managed to get him to safety.

It only took two of us to get him to a chair under a tent to cool off with some water. He was aware of his condition, and we were relieved it wasn't a more serious situation. We only needed two people to help him; we didn't need urgent life care to come flying in. He just needed to be treated with dignity. He just needed shade and a chair. I gave him a Gatorade and some water and made sure he was going to be okay.

The following Saturday, he approached me slowly, calling out, "Jonathan, Jonathan!" He kept calling my name. When he reached me, he took my hand in both of his and shook it, expressing his gratitude for my help.

It was an emotional moment for me. I truly wish more people would act with such kindness. Though I didn't need the thanks, it was his way of showing respect, which filled me with pride.

I felt good knowing I was there to help him during that moment of need. That respect, that sense of fulfillment, is something I carry with me every day.

You may be asking, "So what happens when you've clearly been disrespected? How can I show respect to someone who is not showing me respect?" Your response is dependent upon the situation.

Back in Philadelphia, during a time when I was still drinking and building my team, we had a night out to celebrate our successes. As you're growing a new business, it's vital to make sure you're celebrating, especially the large successes. At that point in time with our group, we were climbing Mount Everest (it seemed), and it was time to celebrate a win.

I told everyone they could come in at 9 a.m. the next day. I thought this would be great; everyone could sleep in, stay out later, and enjoy the celebration. However, that turned into a teaching moment about respect for me as a leader.

The next morning, I arrived at the office, and at 8:50 a.m., no one had shown up. I was hiring straight out of college, and these guys were eight to ten years younger than me. By 9:10 a.m., I heard the back door open. We are all human. Things happen. But when your boss gives you an extra hour to make it into the office and you are still late... nope. It was disrespectful. I extended a kindness, and my team pushed the boundary.

As they walked by my office to get to the main work area, I noticed they had stopped at McDonald's and brought me a couple of breakfast sandwiches. They threw the sandwiches in my direction, clearly sensing I was upset and about to explode.

I thought, *Really? You think a breakfast sandwich is going to win me over?* I put the sandwiches down and said, "When I tell you to come in at 9, I mean be here at 9, not at 9:10. I gave you an entire hour, and you disrespected that by arriving late without letting me know. I came here on time."

That incident stuck with me. I didn't lash out at them, but they understood they had crossed a line. From that point forward, they never took advantage of my kindness again. (And I never saw another free breakfast sandwich... lol.)

That's the lesson: people will take advantage of your kindness and respect if you let them. Once that respect is lost, it can be hard to regain. It's a valuable lesson to learn and is often learned the hard way. After that isolated incident, it never happened again.

Respect is imperative in navigating more monumental actions as well. Reading the gravity of the situation will determine the level of respect both given and allowed to be received. There have been situations where jobs were on the line and the tone was very serious. Respect sets the tone, especially in intense situations where leaders are pressed to be direct, honest, and to the point.

Terminations are an area where respect can completely alter the long-term impact of difficult news. It doesn't matter what industry you're in; anyone losing a job is always going through a tough situation. In some situations, it's self-inflicted, but in others, it may include circumstances that do not have anything to do with an employee's performance. It is vital to show respect and treat people with dignity during these situations. Tough situations handled with respect lighten the blow on those on the receiving end.

It also shows an abundance of respect to put proactive thought into the conversation. You have to be direct, to the point, look them in the eyes, and make sure they understand what you're trying to achieve in that conversation. Respect the impact that these tough conversations will have on the human in front of you. Having a difficult conversation guided by respect will help everyone walk away with understanding and proper closure.

Respect, personally and professionally, should be a goal in any and all interactions on a daily basis. We're not perfect, and sometimes we miss, but if we apply focus (perhaps *Soul Focus*) to respecting the people around us and the environment we are walking into, then we're much more likely to create lasting, connected relationships. When we are able to both give and receive respect authentically, we build bridges of humanity.

CHAPTER 8

Reliable: It Can Make or Break You

RELIABILITY IS NOT JUST about being available 24/7, 365 days a year. For me, it represents stability and support. When we consider the meaning of "reliable," it encompasses being present for someone, ensuring that something can withstand challenges, and helping others walk through life's trials.

The importance of reliability became particularly clear during a time when my family suffered a great loss. My second-oldest brother, Rob, had four kids before he passed away. As discussed previously, after Rob's death, I moved away but recognized the importance of being a dependable figure for everyone, especially for Missy, my brother's widow, and his four kids: Andy, Josh, Evan, and Emily.

Even after relocating to Detroit and later to Philadelphia for my career, I wanted them to know they could rely on me. I aimed to be the uncle they could call on in times of need. Over the years, my family reassured me that my presence brought them comfort. I learned that I did not have to be physically present in order to be a reliable figure in their lives. They could always rely on me to pick up the phone and listen, offer advice, or just be a sounding board for what they were experiencing. I was there, I truly showed up, and focused entirely on them.

I also faced tough moments that tested my reliability. I was honored to give the eulogies for both my brother and my dad. Speaking about the life of someone that you love dearly and will forever grieve for is no easy task. Yet, my family turned to me, and without hesitation, I stepped up. I felt proud to fulfill that role.

This experience made me realize that being reliable felt like a superpower, allowing me to support my family through difficult times. Perhaps this strength emerged as a way to cope with Rob's loss. I committed to nurturing my immediate family while also being there for my extended family as much as possible. I wasn't always perfect. I couldn't make every game or family dinner. But I showed up whenever I could, and they always knew I was just a call away.

My dedication to reliability is reflected in the name of my company, Soul Focus, LLC. It embodies the idea that when you are present, you should be fully engaged, with both your head and your heart. This means being fully in the moment, participating in conversations, and not allowing yourself to get distracted.

Consistency and reliability go hand in hand. One cannot exist without the other. After Rob's passing, I realized that I wanted to become the person who could light up the room for my family. My brother's loss left a hole that could never truly be filled, but I wanted to be a person they could rely on for laughter and joy. I have always aspired to be someone my loved ones could count on, free of judgment. I understand the pain of struggling personally, so I do my best not to judge others because I know what it's like to navigate difficult situations.

Being reliable professionally is critical. Not only is it absolutely necessary in order to gain trust from clients, but it is also a key piece to relationship-building with your team. When I started at Brooksource, I was twenty-seven years old. Over time, I ended up hiring people who were five to seven years younger than me. When I moved to Philadelphia, many new employees were about ten to eleven years younger. It was essential for me to be a reliable leader. They needed to know that I would be there for them in any meeting, to support them, and to help them grow their careers. I wanted them to know that they could call me at any time and I would be there to help them work through their challenges and collaborate with them to find solutions. You must be a reliable leader in order to help build those around you. They cannot learn from you if they cannot rely on you to be there to listen and instruct.

Additionally, clients need to learn about more than just your product. They need to learn that they can rely on you to consistently listen and meet their needs. If you're genuinely trying to build lasting relationships rather than just focusing on a single sale or KPI, they need to know that they can rely on you as a business partner.

Sometimes, clients just want someone who can and will listen to them. Being a reliable resource for communication will go a long way with clients. Make sure they understand that they are always a priority. Simple gestures like always returning a call or email the same day will prove your reliability. You might not even have the answer to their question yet, but the act of circling back to them and letting them know you are working on it creates trust.

As stated earlier, reliability can be like a superpower. Use it to show up for your clients, for your consultants, and for all of the important people in your life. It's amazing when you see what the power of being reliable can do for your outlook. When you become someone that you know others can rely on, you feel a real sense of purpose for being on this planet. Reliability is the attribute that keeps all the other attributes bonded together. Drop the ball on being reliable, and trust can easily erode.

For all the salespeople reading this, when you prepare for meetings with your leaders, consider whether you discuss personal stories or difficulties your managers may have encountered that may not relate to gaining the business or hitting KPIs. Being compassionate, reliable, and present as a leader, and as a listener, for your clients is absolutely essential in setting yourself apart from your competition.

Once your clients trust you due to your reliability, relational friendships and partnerships can form. If you think you can't create these connections and that everything is merely transactional, you're mistaken. If you treat your client interactions like transactions, then you are robbing yourself of the opportunity to create a lasting partnership. Clients tend to stick with you when they know you're there for them.

Early on in my time in Philadelphia, we had a weekend project where some of the consultants didn't show up. In sales, this is a common occurrence. Things go wrong. Sometimes, despite our best efforts, things don't go as planned. This situation not only put our reputation on the line with the manager, but it also jeopardized the entire timeline of the project. Without hesitation, I told him I would be there. I assured him I would work to get candidates right away, but if I had to do the work myself, I was prepared to do so. Although that was not an ideal situation, it did allow me to prove to my client that I was reliable and invested in their success. This builds trust and loyalty.

Being reliable doesn't mean you have to answer the phone 24/7, 365 days a year. It simply means when someone you know, who is in need, calls, you answer. You're present. You show up in whatever way you can to show your commitment.

Reliability is the third corporate CARE attribute within my framework, which I believe every organization in America should adopt. As we put this together, consider that we've established *consistency*. If your company *adapts* to clients' needs, which can shift daily, and you also add the ability to be *reliable*, you are building something valuable.

The main objectives to consider: Is your company's staff consistently reliable? Are they reliably adapting? Are they executing effectively? I will discuss this in more detail later on. When you reach the last chapter, you'll see how this all comes together.

Remember that this principle doesn't apply only to leaders, but to salespeople, and clients alike; it also extends to your peers, coworkers, family members. Every organization should promise reliability to its people, customers, and employees.

Reliability means being responsive when someone truly needs your help. These interactions become moments of truth for you and your organization. Are you going to be the person who doesn't answer the phone, or will you establish a brand known for picking up the phone and being there for clients? This, in summary, encapsulates what it means to be reliable.

So why was "Reliable" so important to have as a part of my CARE Framework?

The term "Reliable" is included because clients in the feedback loop I created consistently mentioned it. They would say, "I choose to work with you because of A, B, and C." Being reliable was always one of those reasons. They knew that my professional success and livelihood depended on my role in building this company. Not being there for my clients, my consultants, or my coworkers would mean that I was literally failing at my job. Reliability was a cornerstone of what I was building. I cannot emphasize enough how important this attribute is when you are building your brand. Regardless of what you are actually selling, your partners need to see you as a reliable person in order to trust you with their business.

You're here 24/7/365, and that's amazing if you're a 24/7 company. However, what if you're not? What if you're supposed to be able to leave work at 5:00, and a client manager calls you at 6:30? Do you answer? Have you switched your mindset to "off the clock"? In the services industry, "off the clock" should not be an option. Our clients and consultants depend on us to be there for them. Hence, the use of, and increase of, chatbots to help with customer-related issues. Technology has made reliability much easier. However, in physical form, you must be able to be there for your clients, consultants, coworkers, and the people in your life you care about the most.

In order to achieve professional success, you must be willing to accept some personal sacrifice. This doesn't mean you need to be tied to your desk 24/7, 365 days a year. We all have responsibilities outside of work hours that need to be managed. Work–life balance is always a teetering scale. Some days will require more from you than others. However, I know that if an important phone call comes in, I step away and respond immediately. I choose to prioritize that urgency and work to be reliable when it matters.

With the dynamics of the workforce changing and the traditional office setting no longer an absolute, reliability should still be at the forefront of your relationship-building. People are seeking more freedom in their lives, moving away from the traditional office environment where one might work forty to forty-five hours a week at a desk. Nowadays, many jobs can be performed virtually from home or have "hybrid" capability. This means that the concept of being accessible 24/7, 365 days a year doesn't necessarily require sitting in a cubicle; it can be done from anywhere.

Building a long-term relationship with clients means being present for them. If a manager calls you on a Saturday at four o'clock and you don't answer, that's not nurturing a relationship; it's merely a transactional mindset aimed at profit. Instead, you should convey to that manager that you're there for them 24/7, 365 days a year.

Consider reliability when you put this commitment into action when a friend needs a ride at 2 a.m. or when a client reaches out because one of your consultants didn't show up. Being available when needed is crucial.

How do I know this matters? Clients don't expect me to be available all the time, but they know that when they call, I will answer. They trust that my demeanor and personality reflect reliability and that I will follow through on their requests. This reliability becomes a superpower.

Being reliable isn't just something you say; it's something you do. It's something you show by action. It's how you help clients realize you are there for them whenever they reach out. You become a reliable leader when you stay after hours and help them improve their skills and sharpen their saw. It's spending a little extra time with your son in the backyard so that he can work on his curveball, or one extra game of PIG so my other son can work on his jumper, when you're tired and all you want to do is go inside and rest for the night. It's making sure you show up and are there for your partner and loved ones.

As I said earlier in this chapter, if you're reliable personally, it should reflect professionally. Focusing on being reliable and understanding its importance in comprehensive relationship-building is one of the keys to long-term success.

CHAPTER 9

Relatable: Do You Understand Your Audience?

IN THIS CHAPTER, I WANT TO discuss the importance of being relatable. As people, we all have a unique background and set of life experiences that make us who we are. Being able to find connections with others through those shared life experiences is the key to being relatable. You may not have grown up in the same area as your neighbor, but maybe you both have three siblings. You didn't go to the same college as your colleague, but you had the same major. These common threads help break down barriers and help us see part of ourselves in others. Being able to connect with others on the basis that somewhere you can find a shared experience or something in common is the very essence of being relatable. The ability to be relatable is extremely important in both personal and professional interactions because it helps build the bridge for authentic, human connection.

Having a genuine interest in leaning in and learning new things makes you much more relatable. Growing up in a small town, I realized that my scope of worldly experience was limited. I needed to broaden my horizons and expose myself to different experiences in order to become more relatable.

Transitioning from a small Catholic school to Central Michigan University and having an internship in a large city near Detroit opened up new perspectives for me. Life experiences like these add to your personal resume and help you relate to people about a variety of topics.

It's essential to step outside your comfort zone and embrace different experiences, knowing that people will come in and out of your life along the way, teaching you valuable lessons. My personal story of when I first learned to tie a fishing knot can be used to connect with someone with a similar passion and lead us into a conversation based on shared interests. In my high school choir, I once performed "Chestnuts Roasting on an Open Fire" in front of about a thousand people at Kellogg Auditorium. It was obviously a very big deal for our school and for me personally. The nerves of singing in front of friends and their families were intense, but sharing that story of being nervous and unsure makes me more relatable. By facing my fear and embracing it, I gained another experience to share with others.

Curiosity fosters learning, allowing me to communicate effectively with individuals across generations. If you're a salesperson reading this book, trying to figure out how to sell your product or connect with clients, consider all the diverse topics that can come into play, such as sports, fishing, farming, fine arts, health and fitness, hunting, handling loss, navigating through a divorce, travel, music, and exploring various cultures, among others.

In my twenties and thirties, I recognized the value of surrounding myself with people who could teach me new things, whether learning to fish for salmon on Lake Michigan or understanding the importance of hard work. The people in my life offered me the opportunity to gain new life experiences, and I was able to use those experiences to become a more relatable, well-rounded person. Using your own life experiences as a catalyst can allow you to connect professionally with people who often want to connect over something beyond relational topics.

I encourage you to grab a piece of paper and a pen. Start writing down everything you've learned, and you may be surprised at how much you can share. When you express knowledge about various topics, even if it's limited, clients will appreciate your willingness to learn, and they'll often start sharing their own experiences, creating a deeper connection.

So, lean into learning new things. I was terrified to sing "Chestnuts Roasting on an Open Fire," but I did it, and my family and friends were proud of me for stepping up. That core memory taught me that relating to people and putting yourself out there can foster a unique human experience.

Professionally, we all share common experiences. Start with building a foundation based on these shared experiences, and you'll find it easier to connect with and understand your audience.

Acknowledge to managers that you understand they receive hundreds of calls every day. I often reminded them, "I know you get a hundred calls a day or a hundred a week. Why did you take mine? I'm aware you have fifteen people coming in to sell you something every week. Why are you listening to me right now?" Set a narrative that they can connect with before diving into your proposal. When you meet with a manager, point out that you recognize they are busy and inundated with salespeople. It's essential to address this situation upfront to create a positive experience with the person you're speaking to.

Pay attention to their office decor and the items on their desk. This isn't snooping; it's about learning who you're talking to. If there are pictures of fish on the wall, for instance, they likely enjoy fishing, so engage them in that topic. In virtual meetings, observe their surroundings and mannerisms, as these can offer personal insights as well.

Being open to learning about other people and different generations is crucial for being relatable. Clients want to buy from someone they know; they don't want to feel sold to by someone insincere. The moment you understand they have limited time, aim to provide them with a return on their time. This shows them that you value their time and that you're not there to waste it.

Emphasize that your priority is to learn first and sell second, and they will appreciate it. That act alone differentiates you from your competition. It was always my client strategy, and it was abundantly successful. Once I communicated my intention, I could see it in the client's face that they appreciated that approach and had not heard it often.

Clients dislike being pressured with statements like, "You have to use our service; it's the best out there." That approach is aggressive and is not conducive to fostering a relationship built on earned trust. Instead, as I've mentioned throughout this book, clients prefer to buy from those they feel a connection with. Sharing your story and your *why* is vital.

I approach getting to know someone like building a friendship, starting with curiosity, asking questions, and finding common ground.

Sometimes, simply being kind can make you more relatable. I've had account executives tell me that a certain manager was unpleasant and would never smile during their meetings. I would respond, "Just wait! I refuse to let anyone leave without smiling." I took that as a personal challenge. I made it my personal mission to bring the right energy to that meeting and find a way to connect with those "hard-to-please" clients.

More often than not, they are not mean people. They are busy, they are tired, and, more importantly, they feel like they've heard the same sales approach a thousand times. Approaching the meeting with the goal of finding areas where you can relate to that manager can break the cycle. This allows you to connect with them personally and creates organic dialogue.

I made a point to tell managers, often in front of my nervous salesperson, "My goal is to make you smile. My goal is to get you to laugh. By doing this, I hope we can build some mutual respect and that you'll realize we're here to learn, not to take." That's really how you create a connection.

When you establish a positive tone and narrative, the manager is likely to feel less like they are being sold to and more like they are genuinely building a relationship with someone they might know for years. As a result, they may be more inclined to buy your product. Consider all the personal experiences you've had in your life that can enhance your professional interactions with managers.

In every communication you have throughout the day, strive to be relatable. Reflect on your past experiences and apply them to your professional interactions. By doing this, you'll foster a sense of connection.

I wasn't a 4.0 student at CMU, and honestly, I didn't want to be. Greatness in a person doesn't come from the pursuit of perfection. People appreciate authenticity; they want to know that you are not perfect. Relatable people are oftentimes the most authentic ones in the room.

I would tell my managers, "Things will not always be perfect. Inevitably, something will go wrong, but know that I am fully committed to addressing it immediately. I will treat any issue like a fire that needs to be put out." If you're a salesperson out there reading this book, set the tone with your managers and be honest and upfront with them. You are not going to be perfect, and not everything is going to go as planned, but you will be there to correct any issues along the way. Make sure the client and anyone involved in the buying process understand that your goal is for them to be happy at the end of the day. Remember, these conversations are relational interactions, not transactional procedures.

Think about this as a leader. Are you supposed to be perfect? Have all the answers? Never make a mistake? Nonsense. You won't be perfect; in fact, you need to share your imperfections. As a leader, it makes you more relatable!

I'm not perfect. When you set that tone, it opens up the possibility for collaboration. You'll find that many clients will thank you for being honest about your imperfections. It's a refreshing approach. There are many who come in claiming they will get everything right, but that isn't a realistic expectation. You set yourself up for failure if you commit to things that are not always within your control. The moment you approach a situation honestly, similar to how you would in a relationship, acknowledging that perfection isn't the goal, you can achieve much more with your interactions.

When I was in more of a sales leader role, I would see it all too often: a salesperson really trying to get through their pitch, but sometimes it felt forced. I used to play rap or country music or tell a joke, getting my account executives singing and dancing in the car before meetings. I wanted them to walk into meetings feeling loose and just being themselves. The more they practiced working on themselves, the more they were able to actually deliver the content they were worried about getting across in the first place. "It's just staffing," I would say. "There's nothing you can say that we can't fix," is what I would tell young account executives, and that is still true today.

This message extends beyond staffing and applies to anyone in the service field. You can't go into a meeting nervous that you're being judged. You must realign your mindset so that you go into a meeting excited. You are being given the opportunity to explore a new relationship and learn more about an existing or future client. It's important to remember that if you're working on and using the rest of the CARE attributes listed in this book, it is quite easy to be relatable.

It's also important to note at this point in the book, as discussed in the introduction, that the goal is to get communications and interactions to a flow state. That flow state is when you are utilizing all twelve of your attributes within a conversation. Getting into a flow state can bring about the "IT Factor," as talked about earlier in the book. When the head and the heart come together, when you're using all these attributes to build a common connection, that's when you've reached a flow state, and true relationships are born.

While I don't give a twelve-CARE attribute survey after every interaction I have, I do think about every one of these attributes before I go into an interaction. While I'm preparing, I will research the personality of, and any knowledge about, the client or the person I'm interacting with to help me formulate a game plan (not an agenda) for which attribute I might have to hit on the most during my interactions that day. Being a chameleon and being able to jump from one attribute to another will allow you to curate the lasting communication that is critical when building a solid relationship.

Hitting a flow state with the hopes of long-term building champions and partners that will work with you throughout your career should be your goal. If they make a sale, that's great; if not, it's not the end of the world. When you continue to approach others with a focus on being *authentic* and *relatable*, doors will open. If your relationship with your clients/potential clients continues to develop, so will additional opportunities. I encouraged my salespeople to go in and be genuine. What makes you unique as a person should be used to your advantage professionally.

I may not have had a perfect 4.0 GPA, but I made up for it in spades with my energy and work ethic. This is what helped set me apart from my peers and made me a standout in my industry. I used these intrinsic parts of myself as a way to relate to clients. When you can express your energy to your clients, it sets the tone for the relationship. Being flawed and real has its own charm. Being open and vulnerable makes me more relatable.

The first time I visited Manhattan was during a layover on the way back from an awards trip to Mexico with Danielle, very early on in my career. At that time, I never imagined I would even get to see Manhattan, especially Times Square. Luckily, our layover was at LaGuardia, and we had enough time to explore.

Since we were staying the night, we decided to head into Times Square. I remember looking up at the buildings in the evening and being blown away.

The atmosphere was vibrant with life. Growing up in Battle Creek, I felt amazed to find myself in Times Square. I called my family to share my excitement. I described how beautiful the buildings looked and how incredible the experience was.

As I stood there, I reflected on all the little things I had accomplished that had led me to this moment: deciding to make that leap from small town to big school and starting over at twenty-six years old, determined to create a better life for myself. All of those choices had somehow led me to Times Square with my amazing wife, realizing this world's a big place.

Little did I know that a few years later, I would be living in Philadelphia and would eventually help to expand East Coast operations to include a Manhattan office (now Eight Eleven's thriving Hoboken market). These full-circle moments in your life are stories worth sharing. Everyone fortunate enough to have been there remembers the first time they saw Times Square. It's a common thread that can be shared, and from it a conversation is born. The possibilities of where that conversation can lead are endless.

I have a good friend who taught me many outdoor skills, like how to shoot a gun, how to tie a proper fishing knot, and my personal favorite, how to salmon fish in Lake Michigan. These were all things I had never done before meeting him. Without even realizing it, our friendship had opened me up to a different way of life. I now understand and know things I would not have known if I had never met him.

I remember a childhood friend who lived on a farm. He would rise at 4 a.m. to feed the cows and watch out for the bull. Whenever I stayed over, I was expected to do the same. It was completely unlike the life I led in my home, but it showed me life in someone else's shoes. None of these experiences seemed relevant at the time, but now I realize how important they are.

All of these little stories are ultimately part of my story, and they add up to an incredibly great one. All of us have experiences unique to our lives, and they make us more relatable to those around us. You are full of experiences and stories that have created a life that clients want to know more about. Shared experiences matter. So as I said before, grab a pen and paper and write down some of your personal stories and experiences, and then start sharing with your managers. Following this path will help you develop and curate the beginnings of a lasting relationship.

Clients want to know more about the person they are considering spending millions of dollars with. By sharing these experiences and connections, we can form relationships with people we never thought we could. This is why I believe it is vital to be relatable and maintain a robust communication flow with others.

It's interesting how even small random things can become conversation starters. For example, I come from the land of Kellogg's, also known as "Cereal City." In the mornings, the air was filled with the scent of cereal. It's true! You could actually smell when they were making Frosted Flakes or Raisin Bran. People often don't believe me, but it was just a part of life there. It's a random fact and detail of my life that, when shared, can immediately ignite a conversation. Managers prefer to do business with people who are open and expressive and can discuss a variety of topics.

This book is not only for the salesperson or account executive who is trying to carve out their success, but it's also for leaders who are seeking to find their voice and platform. Using the CARE program will enable you to become a more effective leader. This program allows you to identify areas of strength and weakness in yourself and your team. Leading by example and working on your own areas for improvement will set the precedent of self-evolution for those around you. You can also learn from each other in this process. Someone who excels in one area can offer advice and counsel for those who need a boost.

As I've mentioned, the CARE Framework is specifically built around twelve attributes. Dedicate January to consistency and then focus on compassion and other attributes throughout the year, one each month. By December, you will come full circle and will find that you have created solid relationships that extend beyond basic client interactions. The number of flow state conversations you achieve will increase dramatically, and the number of deep connections you build will do the same. Referrals will start coming your way. You will have created a network of people who know you and trust your process.

When you leave a great experience in the wake of your client's environment, other clients soon become aware, and the flywheel starts on a successful business and on a meaningful and memorable career. This is where you build promoters. When your clients are promoting you and whatever it is you're selling or providing, then you know you've done your job effectively. You will have built your own billboard and will be remembered for all the right reasons.

By the end of the year, you'll have deepened your connections with people and learned more about them than you ever thought you could. You will have shared more of yourself than you thought possible, and you'll find that your life is richer for it. It all starts with sharing more about yourself rather than just relying on the brochure or elevator pitch in your backpack. If you want to deepen your connections and secure your relationships, stay relatable, and keep sharing your life experiences. Clients actually do care about them.

CHAPTER 10

Enthusiastic: Are You Living the Day?

THIS IS A MENTALITY I HAVE and how I start every single day. In my early forties, I began to fear Father Time. I felt like my life was on the clock, and I yearned for longevity, which prompted me to make significant life changes in order to improve my health.

I emphasize *enthusiastic* because it reflects your attitude and how you approach each day. Having endured so much personal loss, I understand the importance of this mindset. As I have mentioned previously, I was present when my brother, Rob, passed away. This obviously profoundly affected my life. The sense of loss I felt was overwhelming. Watching someone you love, with so much life left in them, slip away highlights how precious life truly is. Every day, I genuinely wake up with this realization. Yes, there are tough days when getting out of bed feels challenging, but I remind myself, *Get up, Jonathan. He can't. You can!*

Live the day. I firmly believe this applies to everyone on the planet. There's no reason not to pause for even a millisecond and appreciate that your heart is beating and your lungs are functioning. This is incredibly important, and I start each day with that gratitude.

You have to find what brings you joy in your day-to-day life and use it to drive your enthusiasm. It is essential to have a "true north" or a passion that guides your day. What's your passion? What's your true north? These things should fuel natural enthusiasm, even if you don't consider yourself enthusiastic by nature.

Your life must be driven by passion, and that passion acts as your navigational point. As mentioned in previous chapters, don't hesitate to share your passion with others. It helps them understand you as a person and connects them to what you are trying to achieve.

My brother, Rob, was one of the most enthusiastic people I have ever met. He had a way of lighting up a room, and I aspired to follow his lead. I saw how his enthusiasm became contagious. If Rob was excited, everyone was excited. I saw what a powerful attribute enthusiasm can be. You have the power to redirect the energy of a conversation. You can command the room. Adding enthusiasm can change the trajectory of a relationship, both personally and professionally. With his loss, I now have the honor of carrying that torch of enthusiasm. I choose to say "get to" instead of "have to." "Have to" feels burdensome, while "get to" shows that it is an honor and privilege.

On a personal and professional level, my mindset shifted from "winning the day" to "living the day" when my dad died. Sitting by his side in hospice for two weeks gave me plenty of time to reflect on how precious life is. Each day I had with him was a gift. We may not have been "winning the day," but each day I was able to share with him was one that we were able to live together. That was the gift. When the time came for him to leave us, I knew my life would change forever. I knew the experience had completely changed my perspective on what *winning* versus *living* meant to me.

That day transformed my mentality from winning the day to simply living the day. Winning implies that each day is a game to be conquered, and that if you somehow haven't won the day, then you have lost. But what did you lose? Even bad days teach us valuable lessons. Challenges and disappointment are part of life's journey, and they build our character. Each day on this planet is a gift, and we should be grateful for the opportunity to live it. It allowed me to shift my enthusiasm for life and its many opportunities into a mindset that guided my path.

Enthusiasm can be seen, heard, and felt. As discussed previously, I learned from my friend and co-founder of the Eight Eleven Group, Ryan Hasbrook, that you should never sit in the lobby while waiting for a client. He taught me that it implies laziness and a lack of readiness. He believed the receptionist was always watching, and you need to demonstrate a sense of enthusiasm in meeting others. It is a piece of advice that always stuck with me and that I continued to share with my own team. Does sitting in the lobby scrolling on your phone send the right message? Providing your client with your undivided attention and enthusiasm will help prove how much you value their business and your relationship.

Passion is also vital. It signifies you have an inherent destination where your vision meets reality. When you share that passion with your clients, they are more likely to want to open up and share more about themselves. This is where you can build some serious synergy.

When you think about being enthusiastic, remember that it reflects on those around you, including managers. They will sense your energy the moment you walk in, which can brighten their day. Your attitude and approach have an impact.

You woke up today, and you should already feel thankful. That's why enthusiasm is one of my core values. Enthusiastic people are remembered, while unenthusiastic ones fade into the background. When was the last time you wanted to buy from someone who lacked enthusiasm? It doesn't happen. So, carry your enthusiasm with you and let your life experiences guide you on that journey.

Don't hesitate to share your enthusiasm with your clients. Enthusiasm is like a positive flow of energy; it's an uplifting emotion that can be beneficial. Clients won't shy away from it; instead, they will perceive it as a strength. Ultimately, being enthusiastic can be powerfully persuasive. If you are enthusiastic about your product and services and passionate about how that can benefit others, then you are far more likely to spark that energy in return.

I've realized that early on in my career, I put too much pressure on myself to "win the day." The truth is, there will simply be days when you don't come out on top. There will be days that challenge you, and you'll need to get up the next day and find your way through them. The idea of consistently winning the day is a fallacy; it just isn't realistic.

So, I asked myself, *What can I do consistently?* The answer is that I can't win every day. However, I can live each day to the fullest, and that is something I can do consistently. I can wake up every morning and start from a place of gratitude. I can take a deep breath and remind myself, *I'm alive and I have the ability to do great things.* That's a consistent starting point, and everything else can follow from that.

By changing my paradigm and choosing to live the day, I've set myself up for success. If I place too many expectations on myself, I'm bound to feel disappointed and lose my enthusiasm. If I don't win the day, I don't want to go to bed feeling like I failed. Instead, I aim to go to bed knowing that I did my best and that tomorrow will provide me with another opportunity to achieve my objectives. Assess, reprioritize, and set those goals for the next day. It's the "live to fight another day" approach. Setting goals for yourself and pursuing those goals with enthusiasm is key to long-term success.

There are a lot of cocky people out there. While attending professional conferences and seminars throughout the years, you inevitably meet people with a tremendous amount of ego. This can be intimidating and off-putting. As the day's meetings blend into the evening's cocktail hours, the tales get taller. Everyone believes they have landed the largest clients, that they have mastered the art of the sale, and that their way is the superior way. I would often ask myself, "Is this person genuinely enthusiastic about what they do, or are they more focused on the perception of their importance?"

If we asked their clients, what would their feedback be? Do you think they would say that this person has passion and enthusiasm for what they do? Have they worked to build genuine human connections, or have they worked to hit a number? Are they taking care of their clients' needs, or are they so focused on their "success" that they don't even realize that there are additional opportunities available within that organization? Who's really putting the client first? Who's teaching their people first so that professionally they thrive? Those are the types of discussions I want to hear after 10:00 p.m. at a networking event.

Life is about being true to yourself. In that pursuit, you will find both success and failure, and they are both equally important to your development as a person. But if you're only chasing key performance indicators (KPIs), you're likely in it for the wrong reasons. Conversely, if you're focused on building relationships, you're pursuing the right goals. Having a genuine enthusiasm for an event, or meeting someone new, or learning something new is vital to building lasting relationships.

What does genuine enthusiasm look like? Entering situations with curiosity and having a few starter questions ready to go shows enthusiasm. Walking in with a smile on your face and following the natural flow of conversation with eye contact and nodding your head in agreement or understanding reflects enthusiasm. Inflection in what you're talking about shows both passion and enthusiasm. It keeps people engaged with the subject and makes them want to hear more. People can sense a genuine interest vs. a manufactured one. Enthusiastic people seek to earn and never think they deserve. Enthusiastic people can light up a room, and people who light up the room are people who are remembered.

How do we keep the enthusiastic mentality of "living the day" when the days are tough? Simply being grateful for the fact that you are here and healthy can be helpful. There will be times when you feel low, alone, overworked, or stressed. But the important thing is that you're still here. You can still wake up and hear the birds. You still have the ability to change course and create new opportunities for yourself.

As I mentioned earlier in this chapter, it is important to identify the small things in life that bring you joy and use them to fuel your enthusiasm. It can be as simple as your love for your morning cup of coffee. If that is one of life's little moments that brings you happiness, then celebrate it. Buy a special mug. Try a new creamer. Take a few minutes every morning to let yourself enjoy it.

For me, one of the most beautiful sounds in the world is when I take my dog out in the morning and listen to the birds chirping. It's a small joy that allows me to adjust my mindset to that of gratitude. My gratitude helps build my enthusiasm for the day and the tasks ahead of me. How do you make sure you experience that every single day? I suggest journaling. Admittedly, I need to become more consistent with journaling, but it does help when trying to keep an enthusiastic mindset. Writing down all the positive things in your life that you have going for you helps keep things in perspective when you find yourself stuck in the daily grind.

My goal is to wake up and journal every day. I started this practice as a way to help manage my anger (yep, we've all got our issues), but I have found that journaling has also helped with gratitude, perspective, and my ability to clearly lay out my intentions for the day. Journaling has helped me significantly, and it is a personal growth tool that I highly recommend to others.

Write down how you're feeling. Make it a habit to record one positive feeling every morning. It can be work-related or something in your personal life relating to your wife, husband, or your kids. It doesn't matter what it is; just write down one positive feeling you have. Instead of reaching for your phone, reach for your thoughts and put them on paper. You have just created a positive thought to start your day. Positivity and enthusiasm go hand in hand. If you are starting from a positive place, then enthusiasm will follow. This will make the challenges of the day easier to face. You will be far less likely to become overwhelmed when you start your day from a place of positivity.

Building a relationship with a client isn't solely about financial gain; it's about creating a network of mutual support. If you do this successfully, you will have built a tremendous foundation on which to base your business. You will not just have "clients," you will have true partners and promoters. Your enthusiasm in seeking that partnership will determine the level of success.

Walking into a meeting with a positive attitude and leading with enthusiasm will have you being remembered for all the right reasons. Enthusiasm leaves a lasting impression! This holds true when thinking about the service you're selling or the product you're trying to get your client to purchase. If you're not enthusiastic about the company you work for, the service you provide, or the product you hold in your hand, then you're in the wrong line of work.

Clients want to buy from salespeople who are enthusiastic about the company they work for, the brand they represent, and the product they're trying to deliver. Clients can see from a mile away when a salesperson is unenthusiastic, and such salespeople will never go far. Stay enthusiastic about your product, about the company you work for, and about your brand. If you're not, you need to question if it's time to explore a new path.

This is also why it's so important for leaders to display enthusiasm for teaching, coaching, and mentoring their teams. As I stated before, enthusiasm is contagious, and a person with it can light up a room. It can also help ignite the dreams and professional goals of your salespeople. If you're a leader reading this book, make sure you lead with an enthusiastic nature. Your enthusiasm will set the tone for staff who will be looking to you for guidance on how to succeed professionally. Enthusiasm is a key component for relationship-building and personal fulfillment.

CHAPTER 11

Execution: Are You Doing What You Said You Would?

I LEARNED EARLY ON THAT if you tell people you are going to do something, you'd better follow through. If you don't, you risk becoming completely unreliable and untrustworthy. Being able to execute is a fundamental part of building a relationship based on respect and trust. If you take on a task, then those around you must be able to count on you to complete that task thoroughly. You cannot make a commitment and then not follow through without consequences. It's understood that you need to work hard and execute on the commitments you make.

You are only as good as your word. If your word has become riddled with indecision, if it lacks a consistent tone and sense of urgency in response, then your ability to execute is definitely lacking. Oftentimes, you will see people who struggle with consistency, struggle with execution as well. When I developed the CARE Framework, those were two attributes, frankly, I identified as areas for improvement for myself. I'm a maverick thinker, which means I can get easily sidetracked. I had to build up a consistent nature in my daily routine that allowed me to focus on the execution.

When I was starting over at twenty-six, I recognized that I needed to create a new vision for myself and begin executing a new plan. I was determined to rebuild my life.

I had many skeptics. Not everyone believed I was ready to start a new venture. At that point, I manifested a new vision for my career and my life, and I have never looked back.

So, I wrote a plan to help expand Brooksource. I reached out to Ryan and expressed my desire to start the first satellite market. I devised a strategy to start from the ground up. I could have chosen a different path. I could have found a position in an established market, making a comparable salary to my previous position. I chose to take a risk and start something new because I saw the unlimited potential in executing my plan.

If you've manifested a plan, you have to execute. Every move you make needs to be intentional. You must always work with the end goal in mind in order to execute. This is a vital part of my core values and the CARE program. I make it a priority to do as I say, especially when I have a goal in mind. I strive to achieve those goals through the power of execution. For instance, when I woke up at forty, weighing 248 lb. (to be precise), I realized that I was completely unhealthy, and I needed to make some life changes.

I executed a plan by putting a picture of myself in front of my treadmill along with my target weight. I began running every morning, and gradually, the weight started to come off. It would have been very easy to walk past that treadmill every morning. I could have come up with an excuse not to use it every day if I tried. I made the choice to hold myself accountable and stay committed to the plan. I was determined not to let my health become a detriment to my life. A plan without execution is a broken promise. I refused to break that promise to myself and was able to reach my target weight.

I've been manifesting my goals from a young age. In fact, I can vividly recall realizing in the sixth grade that I would someday help start a company and help others achieve their goals. I knew then that pursuing a business degree was my path to fulfilling that vision. I couldn't have predicted exactly how that would come to pass, but I knew if I continued to set goals and execute, I would find my path.

I didn't expect to help start a market from the ground up, but I'm grateful for the opportunity that Ryan and Jeff offered me when I joined the team. The company was still quite small at this point. I believe I was employee number seven or eight at the time. We were all taking a risk with this new endeavor. This opportunity was everything I needed at that point in my life. It allowed me to execute a new vision for myself and begin anew.

The ages of twenty-six and twenty-seven were particularly challenging for me. It was a time of tremendous change, both personally and professionally. I had to push myself to grow. I had to adapt to my new circumstances and set goals for myself that would keep me moving forward. I did not want to disappoint those who were counting on me, but more importantly, I didn't want to disappoint myself. I knew I had been given a huge opportunity, and the only way it would succeed was through the power of execution. It was my responsibility to chart my own course and stay on that course until I reached my goals.

Execution is something to be valued in your personal relationships as well. When you make a commitment to be there for someone, you absolutely must follow through. If I tell a friend or family member that I will be there for them, then I make sure I am there and give them my full attention.

I have a close friend who often needs help around his house, and he knows he can count on me. While I sometimes joke about his lack of skills, that's what friends are for. Friends should support each other and execute when needed. Execution creates reliability. Reliability creates trust. As you have progressed through this book, you can see that the outlined attributes all work together. When applied to your daily life, you will see the improvement in your human connections.

Professionally, my clients understood that I would follow through on my promises because I made sure they knew my motivation. I launched that office because I wanted to help others grow in their careers. I believed I could lead people and sell effectively.

To achieve that, consistency was essential. Consistency and execution go hand in hand. You cannot execute well without being consistent, and vice versa. These two elements have been foundational for me, and they play a crucial role in all thriving professional relationships.

Clients will quickly lose trust in you if you cannot execute effectively.

Understanding the significance of executing on my promises wasn't just important for me; it was vital for the team. There was never an "I" when referring to the offices—it was always a "we" mentality. We were building it together. We all had to execute our part in order for the business to be successful. As their leader, it was my responsibility to set the standard. I encouraged them to approach each day with the mindset to speak up, share their opinion, and together we'd build the market and create our vision for all of us.

There is no greater fulfillment than knowing you've executed key tasks within a day. It is the compilation of a series of small victories that leads to ultimate success. Knowing that you are working on the process and continuing to complete tasks that will take you one step closer to your goal is the win.

Executing a to-do list and accomplishing all the items on it makes for a great day. Moreover, if you can incorporate personal goals and work toward those as well, then you will find your days to be far more productive and fulfilling.

Execution is not often immediate. It is the commitment to creating a plan in order to achieve a goal and working until you have the plan across the finish line. Clients want to know what you're doing after the call ends. They may or may not understand your behind-the-scenes process, but they are expecting a deliverable plan of action from you.

In the staffing industry, it's crucial to update clients about your efforts, such as sharing that you made a specific number of phone calls and conducted various interviews to narrow down the candidate pool. It's important to inform them that you have internal interviews coming up and hope to present a candidate by a certain deadline. These benchmarks will vary by industry, but the universal key here is communication. The more quickly you can communicate those improvements to your client, the more impressed they will be with your overall experience and product delivery.

Sharing the amount and scope of work you're doing for clients demonstrates that you are actively engaged and invested in their success. The reality is that even if you execute everything according to plan, you may still fall short. The client might go with a different vendor. Understand that your efforts were not a total loss. Clearly communicating and executing a plan with your clients proves that you are dependable and trustworthy. They will be more inclined to offer you additional opportunities in the future because you have proven that you are a reliable resource.

It's crucial to share both execution and accomplishments, as well as the moments when you fall short. This demonstrates integrity. Let me emphasize: execution and accomplishment, or the lack thereof, should always be shared because it shows integrity. If you don't achieve your goal but put in maximum effort, explain that! Communicate how hard you tried and that you came up just short; that builds integrity.

Nobody is perfect, so it's important to share those imperfect moments. This example doesn't show a lack of execution; it shows you executed to the maximum and took a firm initiative to make sure you hit client expectations. You explained your work effort in real time (showing maximum execution) and have proven that you are willing to continue to work hard to earn their business. This continued pattern will ultimately lead to additional opportunities. This concept is essential to the corporate CARE equation.

Execution is the final core CARE attribute that every company should have on its website. Companies that demonstrate *consistency, adaptability, reliability, and execution* are the ones that are truly standing out and who CARE more than their competition.

Clients, customers, colleagues, and family members place their trust, money, and faith in you. You cannot afford to let them down. You must sharpen your skills every day. Becoming complacent leaves the door open for your competitors. If you aren't working to execute, there is always someone waiting to step up to the task.

Companies that consistently execute, on a daily basis, will foster brand loyalty, which is the highest measure of future success for both organizational and personal brands. If you're trying to grow your company and struggling with execution, that could be why you're not making progress.

When you promise a client that you will do something, you must follow through. Otherwise, that client may see you as unreliable, which can damage your relationship. It's important to share your experiences and execute effectively. Overpromising and underdelivering is a common sales mistake. Don't let your eagerness to land the deal lead you to fall short and disappoint your client. You must learn to set realistic expectations so that you can consistently deliver what you promise. As a leader, this is a process you need to practice and preach!

This tends to be a common downfall for "people pleasers" (I count myself in this category as well). In the moment, of course, we want to say yes. We want to say that we will be able to do everything the client is asking of us on the spot. However, without stopping to assess if you are actually equipped to execute their requests, you are putting yourself in a position to let your client down. They will be far less disappointed by you clearly laying out your limitations and setting realistic expectations than they will be by you failing to meet theirs.

By setting clear expectations before trying to please others, you can avoid going overboard and keep yourself in check. This applies to your relationships with clients, your spouse, your children, and your friends. Establishing these expectations can help you manage that aspect of your interactions more effectively.

Let's break down the concept of people-pleasing. There's nothing inherently wrong with wanting to please others, but it's important to consider whether that's truly what your clients need. Do they want you to make them happy, or do they need you to execute tasks effectively?

People pleasers often seek to keep the peace, but that isn't always possible or practical. The CARE Framework is designed to help you become sharper as a person and as a professional. Inevitably, you will continue to face obstacles and challenges throughout your life. Having developed deeper relationships based on consistency and trust will allow you to better navigate those waters without having to make unrealistic commitments.

I actually learned from one of my clients that our competition was sharing the amount of work they were putting into each requirement at the end of every day. I saw the window of opportunity that would open if we maintained clear and concise communication all throughout the sales process.

Clients don't know what happens once we hang up the phone. I understand how hard we're working, but do they? We diligently call hundreds of people to find the right candidates for our clients. However, we weren't communicating how much effort went into presenting a single résumé. After the call, clients would often receive a résumé three days later, but they had no idea what went into that process.

For instance, there might have been 110 phone calls, thirty bios reviewed, fourteen internal discussions, and three final interviews before we presented them with their ideal candidate. From their perspective, it might seem like the résumé just appeared out of thin air. The more you share this data, the more managers understand how hard you're actually working to execute.

This principle applies not only to recruitment but also to product sales. Managers want to know what you have done to enhance your product. They ask, "Why is your product going to help me? Why should I buy it in bulk now?" There are countless variables that influence whether someone chooses your service or product.

Ultimately, it comes down to whether they need it and whether you have put in enough effort to make them want yours over someone else's. By sharing your work and showing how much you've invested in their project or environment, you convey your level of execution and commitment. Staying consistent in your messaging and energy will allow you to continue to earn additional opportunities for partnership.

I'm a big "silver linings" person. I believe there is something good to be found in the darkest of hours. It's not always clear to see at the time, but once you are able to take a step back and reflect, you often realize there is a positive takeaway.

As I mentioned earlier in this book, I lost my brother, Rob. It was one of the most devastating things that has ever happened to me, but the worst day of my life turned out to be one of the best days of my life. It changed every aspect of who I am for the better. I could have gone down a darker path, and I'm not sure I would still be here. So, while that was the most painful day of my life, it also became one of the greatest because it changed the trajectory of my life. I have no doubt that his loss was the catalyst for my choices moving forward.

We recently marked the twenty-fifth anniversary of his passing. The men in my family typically go golfing together every year on the anniversary as a way to celebrate his life. Rob loved golf and was actually a golf pro. We do it to come together and share our memories while participating in one of his favorite hobbies. This past year, I shared my perspective on his loss with members of my family, including three of his four adult children.

When I shared this with them, they were a bit shocked, but they understood. They could see it in my eyes. I told them, "He's with me; he's with us right now. He's standing on this course with us. He's right next to me. He's right next to you." I truly believe that. I feel his presence. I always feel him rooting me on.

Sometimes, it feels like he's within me. I haven't really shared this with anyone, but there are moments when I vividly remember listening to Pink Floyd or Neil Diamond (he loved Neil Diamond) while driving with Rob. While I drove, he'd usually be drinking, and I'd look over at him, just enjoying the music.

Now, I find myself glancing at the empty passenger seat in my car, and I can almost feel him sitting there.

That sensation drives my story and my motivation. It's a major reason why I work so hard. After losing Rob, a lot of things came into focus for me. I knew I had big dreams and that chasing them would be a challenge. We all have one life to live, and every day is precious. Nothing is guaranteed. I had to have a plan and work to execute the plan in order to reach my goals. As I mentioned earlier, execution without a plan is a broken promise. Don't break promises to anyone important in your life, including yourself.

Execution requires full commitment. There is no "corner-cutting" in proper execution. It's the old saying: "Do it right or don't do it at all." Do not commit to something you cannot execute. Lay out a realistic plan, continue working that plan, and reach the benchmarks you have set for yourself. Clients will respect the communication and work ethic, and people in your personal life will know they can always turn to you. Continued communication is a key element of execution. Checking in and circling back both reflect on your ability to follow through.

Every day when you set your goals, execution must be a part of the formula. This practice builds consistency and trust in relationships. If you violate that trust by continuing to make commitments you can't fulfill, then you will lose integrity. Once that is lost, it is extremely difficult to move forward in a functioning partnership. Execution reflects your ability to create a plan of action and then work that plan with the goal of establishing trust through meeting the needs of your client. For leaders, this is critical to ingest. Think about a lack of consistency for a common vision or goal. If you're lacking consistency, then you're also lacking in execution. How many people will follow a leader without a plan of execution? Remember, as a leader, others put their careers in your hands. They want to trust in you. As a leader, execution builds trust.

CHAPTER 12

Eagerness: Can Clients See
Your Sense of Urgency?

WHERE DOES EAGERNESS COME FROM, personally? Eagerness can be observed in body language and heard in our voices. It can be visualized like many other attributes. Eagerness is high energy and displays a sense of urgency to learn, grow, and uncover as much as you can in every conversation you have. For me, my eagerness was instilled by my brother.

My brother, Rob, was an entrepreneur who aspired to be a millionaire by the time he turned thirty. I believed in him, and I knew that he believed in himself. He taught me that you need to have a sense of urgency to unleash your full potential each day. I remember how every summer, when I came home, he would knock on my door at 6:30 a.m., ready to start the day.

I would be out in the car just ten to fifteen minutes later, and we would head off to the construction site, working many nights past dinner. We spent the entire day together, went to lunch together, and returned home together. He constantly emphasized the importance of striving to work harder than everyone else and putting in more effort. His words stuck with me.

I also want to give credit to my dad. He worked in the supermarket industry, and every Friday, while my friends went out to hang out, I would join him at work, stocking shelves (as mentioned previously). I loved that experience. It was the coolest thing to me. Through my dad and brother, I learned that the work never stops; the shelves always need to be stocked. I became eager to learn about why that was necessary and started to understand the concepts of supply and demand. This eagerness drove my desire to acquire new skills and apply them to my daily life.

Throughout those summer months, I felt a strong eagerness, not complacency. Rob was incredibly ambitious. At one point, he was building a golf course while also managing to be a professional golfer. Despite the tremendous stress of supporting four kids, his eagerness taught me that it could be a major strength if utilized correctly.

Sometimes, eagerness can be misinterpreted. It can come off as being pushy or aggressive. To keep that eagerness in check and set the right tone, use curiosity. When you are eager to learn, it helps to ask secondary questions, which shows your genuine interest. Interest draws people in and makes them more open to sharing.

I often see this principle in sports. While watching my son play baseball, I notice that as the pitcher prepares to throw the ball, players are instructed to take a step with every pitch. That little movement illustrates their readiness and sense of eagerness for the next play.

It's the same in life. You should always be ready and eager for your next interaction or opportunity. By proactively adopting a mindset of urgency, you prepare yourself for reactive situations. You may think: *I had already anticipated that*, which allows you to respond effectively.

Eagerness is significant because it shows that you are committed to achieving your goals. Eagerness will always be a part of me. I will always be eager to learn, to help others, to be reliable, and to show curiosity and compassion. I am eager to take focused action across the board and share this book with everyone, along with all my vulnerabilities. All of this came from my collective life experiences and the realization that life wouldn't hand me anything. My dad worked tirelessly until he could no longer work, without any retirement to show for it. It taught me that every day, you have to get up and do the job.

I found that you tend to develop a sense of urgency when you grow up without a lot of money. This sense becomes crucial, especially when you're a teenager trying to help your family by putting food on the table and covering some bills. That reality builds eagerness quickly. You are eagerly working toward a more prosperous future.

Professionally, this translates to a mentality of "whatever it takes." This mentality is essential, especially in the service industry, sales, or leadership roles. If you lack this mindset, you might be in the wrong field.

Whatever it takes means being reliable when the phone rings! It means you are eager to address any matters that arise, regardless of their magnitude. Clients want to work with people who prioritize their needs and demonstrate a true sense of urgency. You must be eager not only to earn their business, but also eager to put in the work to maintain and grow it.

This principle also holds true for leaders. Effective leaders will have a sense of urgency and eagerness to teach. An eagerness to coach allows your salespeople the ability to open up to you and share their struggles and stresses. Eagerness shows your people you're ready to go to battle with them, and that can make all the difference in the world. It cultivates loyalty and trust from those around you.

I want you to think of every day as an interview. If you keep that in mind, eagerness will remain front and center in your actions. If you don't show eagerness during an interview, you won't get the job. Many people forget this principle and become complacent. Clients can sense that complacency, too.

You must bring your best self to every interaction; clients can see it and feel it. Nonverbal cues of eagerness matter. Staying attentive and engaged during meetings is crucial. Making a point to jot down notes shows the client that the details matter to you. It also helps you stay organized and allows you to have those critical details at your fingertips for the follow-up phone call or future meetings. These small actions reflect your eagerness as a professional.

How quickly do you return communications? If you say, "I'll get right back to you," that should mean immediately, not five hours later. It means you are committing to prioritizing this urgent matter above whatever else you were working on. Follow through and stay true to your word. That's how you show a sense of urgency and eagerness.

If you integrate all these attributes, including consistency and eagerness, in your interactions, you will build memorable partnerships that people will appreciate. That appreciation will lead to strong relationships that will stand the test of time.

If a client calls you on a Friday at 5:55 p.m. and you suspect there may be an issue, not answering the call would lack integrity. It's the people who stay after hours and do whatever it takes who demonstrate eagerness.

This is what clients are looking for. As you prepare for your next business meeting, be prepared to take notes. If you're walking into the lobby, engage with the receptionist. It's crucial to execute this engagement at every level.

Incorporating eagerness into both your personal and professional life will show others that you have a genuine sense of urgency and are interested in their matters. That is the essence of eagerness.

If you're eager, people remember you. You have to be eager to learn from everyone around you at all times! Being kind to everyone that you interact with—from the Uber driver, to the receptionist, to the CEO—can lead to new opportunities. Each interaction can lead to an open door for both you *and the* person you're interacting with. You never know who they know, and vice versa! It's a people-helping-people approach.

Lead with kindness and eagerness to learn and connect. If more people engaged in that kind of attitude, the world would be a better place. That's what this entire book is about. If you work to be better from a human perspective and treat people with respect, everything else in life will fall into place.

If you focus on these twelve attributes and aim to reach a flow state, the rest will take care of itself. Be clear about your *why*. Let others know who you are so they aren't caught off guard by your mannerisms or your intentions. Let them understand your goals. Yes, you might be trying to sell something, but only after they're ready to engage with you.

When I first started with the company in 2002, I was eager to prove myself. I was eager to achieve success. Everything I have been able to accomplish professionally has been a direct result of my eagerness.

You have to run toward your fears and use eagerness as motivation. I relied heavily on this mindset to achieve my goals. I was afraid to open a Detroit market. I was afraid to move to Philadelphia and head up East Coast operations. What outweighed my fear was my eagerness to see what I was capable of. Use your fears to catapult you into a different mindset. Instead of *What if this goes wrong?* ask yourself, *What if this goes right?* Eagerness will help keep you on a path to success.

If you're struggling to find your own sense of direction, I hope this book helps you discover your purpose. For me, my priorities are my wife and my children. It took me a while to realize this. At thirty, I might have said my career was my priority. At thirty-five, maybe even forty, I could have thought the same. However, my mindset changed between the ages of forty and fifty, which shifted my perspective. Now, my focus is on being a great husband and father, with everything else coming second.

I've always believed that if you succeed in these personal areas, you will naturally grow professionally. That's why my tagline is "personal growth for professional success." You won't achieve professional success without first developing personally. Who you are professionally is an extension of who you are personally. You need to grow personally in order to achieve professional growth.

How do you find eagerness when you're physically or mentally burnt out? It's not easy, but there are things you can do to realign yourself and get back on track. It's important to be in tune with your needs and allow yourself to prioritize those needs. If you feel physically spent, start looking at your day and target your sleep habits. Work to eliminate the scrolling an hour before bed. It's amazing what a few more hours of sleep can do for your overall health and attitude.

If it's a mental burnout, then it's time to evaluate what is draining your energy. Is your work–life balance off? Do you need to find time in your day or week to set aside for an activity that brings you joy? Sometimes something as simple as prioritizing an outdoor walk or a few minutes of reading can help you reset mentally. Once you have poured back into yourself, you will find the eagerness to pour into others.

Eagerness demonstrates your willingness to learn, adapt, share your failures, and accept whatever comes your way. If you're struggling and feel stuck, tap into that eagerness. How can you do that? Start by going back to the foundational aspects of your life that are positive. A great practice is to write down one positive thing every day. If you journal about these positive moments, you'll navigate challenges more effectively. By working through your experiences and using a positive outlook, you can use eagerness as a powerful tool to move forward.

CONCLUSION

Let's Wrap This in a Bow!

SO THERE YOU HAVE IT: my twelve CARE attributes that have framed my personal life and professional career. You have read my personal stories along with my professional teachings on each attribute within my CARE Framework. You're now more well-versed and equipped to create flow-state conversations! Your chance to create those "IT Factor" moments. You now possess the framework to truly work on human improvement, which I refer to as "the daily treadmill for human improvement."

What's going on in your mind? How do you present yourself? By utilizing my CARE Framework and focusing on these twelve attributes, you can achieve a flow state both personally and professionally, leaving lasting impressions on those you interact with daily. Building up your advocates and promoters into champions and partners through the amazing experiences they have while working with you. Let's bring it back into focus.

What's your core CARE equation:

C: _____

A: _____

R: _____

E: _____

Which attribute is your God-given talent or strength?

Which attribute(s) do you need to focus on the most to improve your overall score?

After reading this book, you can now look at these attributes, look inward at yourself, and uncover which attributes you truly exhibit and are most comfortable with. What's your premier attribute? What attributes do you know you need to work on? What's your CARE performance score? If you're hovering around an 8 or 9, I can promise you that the other attributes you're strong at will help you improve your weaker areas.

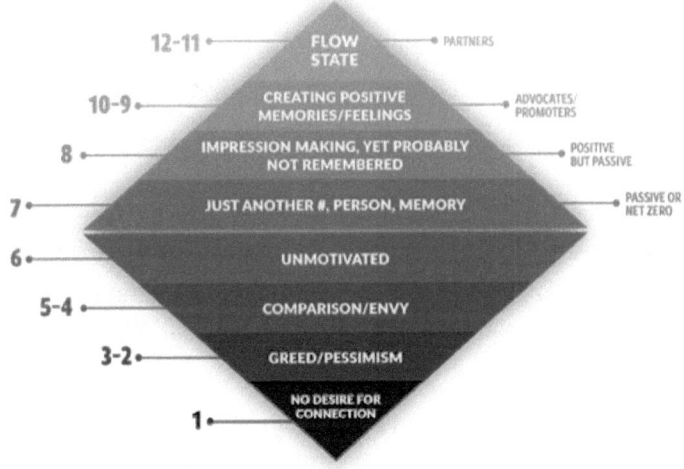

From an organizational perspective, you now have a structured approach that can be applied within your organization. This framework embodies CARE, the equation being: **consistently adaptable**, **reliable**, and **executing** on your word. All reputable companies should aspire to this standard of service. All employees looking to enhance their relationship-building skills should incorporate this framework into their goals. Organizations and leaders should embrace this as part of their ultimate objectives.

Embracing our "perfect imperfections" is essential. It demonstrates our humanity and reassures us that it's okay for things to go wrong. Engage in conversations with your managers and coworkers, sharing who you are and the reasons behind your communication style. Embrace personal growth and use it to push yourself professionally. This is all part of harnessing human improvement. Greatness in a person is not in pursuing it. It's about true purpose without worrying about perfection. Live the day! It's not going to be perfect, navigate it with a positive mindset, kindness, and good will come your way. Or simply, you'll just be a better person. Nothing wrong with that!

Make time each day to express gratitude for what you have, both personally and professionally. Avoid seeking greatness as a goal, because doing so creates unnecessary pressure. I have no agenda to be great, because that implies I will have mastered something. Life is not to be mastered; it is to be experienced. My agenda is simply to live, learn, and be as kind and understanding as possible.

Let me be very clear that while it is so important to live the day, you still must adopt a "whatever it takes" mentality for that day! Life is challenging, and resilience is necessary. You must develop mental toughness. The attributes I've discussed are not negative in nature because that does not foster human growth. While you need to be mentally tough to overcome adversity and prevent external challenges from overwhelming you, remember to confront your fears head-on. Tackle the elephant in the room by explaining the *why* behind your actions and how you can enhance your CARE Framework and your performance score.

If you rate yourself a seven or an eight, collaborate with those you interact with most and ask for their feedback. This serves as a great teamwork exercise. There's always room for improvement. I am still in a state of improvement. I believe that we should all be in a state of improvement as long as we are on this earth. Every day presents us with opportunities to learn and grow. Commit to being a student for life. Remember that perfection is not unattainable. However, the more you care and apply these attributes, the better your interactions with others will be. You will have more success in your professional outcomes, and your organization will thrive. You will also feel a greater sense of fulfillment at the end of each day because you will be connecting with others on a deeper level.

Why this book was so important for me to write and share with the world is simple: every single person has faced struggle. Every person has felt loss, and perhaps you recognized some of your own while reading these pages. Everyone has had, or will have, a medical issue to overcome or fight through at some point in life. This book is for you—to help you realize that struggles can be harnessed and transformed into strength.

Take your medical worry, battle, and hopefully victory, and share your story. Take your loss, and the pain of rebuilding yourself afterward, and share that story, too. A vice or an addiction can be overcome and retold as a source of strength. Doing this requires a focused mindset, determination, and a willingness to improve every day. The twelve attributes woven throughout each chapter are designed to help you build strength, overcome struggle, turn pain into power, and find purpose in building authentic connections—connections that can grow into meaningful professional partnerships.

As a leader, it is important to create a highly accountable environment while still fostering a workplace where people feel comfortable being themselves and striving toward shared goals. It should also be a place where your team can celebrate successes along the way. You don't want your people to feel as if they can't be authentic or that you're constantly looking over their shoulders. That is the heart of this book: the more authentic and relatable you are, the more you will ultimately get out of your team.

Now, with Soul Focus, LLC and soulfocusmindset.com, I am able to help organizations from coast to coast. My framework for Soul Focus, as you have read, is personal growth that leads to professional success. You will see that you are able to achieve more successful outcomes when you apply Soul Focus to the activities that are directly in front of you. This is the foundation of my dream. I am building this company to help *leaders* realize that being *authentic* and *relatable* can truly harness the best versions of themselves and the highest possible levels of success for both themselves and their teams.

I want to express my immense gratitude to everyone who took the time to read this book. I hope you found value in it and discovered areas for your own improvement. May this inspire you to move forward with your own vision, recognizing that you are limitless. Each day is an opportunity to be thankful for simply being alive. By applying the three C's of consistency, compassion, and curiosity, you can begin to lay the foundation for genuine human improvement.

Finally, to my beautiful wife, Danielle, and my amazing boys, Tristan and Logan, I thank you guys from the bottom of my heart. None of this would be worth it if I didn't have your love and support. Danielle, you have always been my rock and my sense of reason. Thank you for everything you've done to support me and my career, vision, and goals. I would also like to thank you for holding it down with the boys during all my crazy years of travel. I know how hard you worked to help raise them into fine young men, and I am so proud of them.

I hope you enjoyed the book, and I look forward to hearing from you at my next keynote. Share with me what your premier Core CARE Equation looks like or what your core attribute would be. I'd love to hear from you! I'm excited to see how you all apply the insights from this book. Thank you once again for reading!

THANK YOU FOR READING MY BOOK!

LET'S CONNECT!

Scan the QR Code:

I appreciate your interest in my book and value your feedback, as it helps me improve future versions. I would appreciate it if you could leave your invaluable review on Amazon.com with your feedback. Thank you!